MARY FORD

A CAKE
FOR ALL
SEASONS

ACKNOWLEDGEMENT

Mary Ford acknowledges with grateful thanks the assistance of Pat Cockayne in making some of the flowers in this book.

MARY FORD TUBE NUMBERS SHOWING THEIR SHAPES

·	•	●	●	●	✳	✸	✴	✹	✺	⌒
0	1	2	3	4	5	7	42	43	44	57

The above are all the icing tubes used in this book. Please note that these are Mary Ford Tubes, but comparable tubes may be used. All the tools and equipment required to complete the cakes and floral decorations in this book are obtainable from the Mary Ford Cake Artistry Centre, 28-30 Southbourne Grove, Bournemouth, Dorset, BH6 3RA, England, or local stockists.

Copyright 1990 Mary Ford Publications Limited.
Published by Mary Ford Publications Limited,
28-30 Southbourne Grove, Southbourne, Bournemouth,
Dorset BH6 3RA, England.

Printed and bound by Arti Grafiche Vincenzo Bona, Turin, Italy

ISBN 0 946429 08 1

Mary Ford stresses the importance of all aspects of cake artistry, but gives special emphasis to the basic ingredients and unreservedly recommends the use of Tate and Lyle Icing Sugar.

Contents

AUTHOR

MARY FORD is internationally known for her superb cake artistry skills and in this book she also displays her considerable versatility and expertise in basic cake making. She has been involved in all aspects of baking throughout her long and successful career, which included the practical day to day supervision of her cake and tea shop in Bournemouth, England. Mary has more recently expanded her work into an exciting new range of craft and cake artistry books and cake decoration equipment which bring her skills to a wider public. All the books are based on the famous Mary Ford pictorial, step-by-step training method which Mary devised for her Cake Artistry School and which has proved so successful.

Her husband Michael, himself an experienced cake-maker, has collaborated closely with Mary and has taken all the photographs in this book.

INTRODUCTION

THIS lavishly illustrated, step-by-step guide provides the cake-maker with all the inspiration needed for imaginative and exciting baking and decorating throughout the year. Its invaluable, practical pictorial format takes the reader progressively through every stage essential for successful results.

Each month Mary Ford offers one of her own favourite, tried and tested tea-time recipes.

There are also a host of inventive new and traditional designs and seasonal decorations for every occasion, together with instructions for making beautiful sugar flowers and realistic fruits and nuts for celebration cakes. Cake artistry at its best is illustrated by the large, beautifully coloured photographs of the finished cakes.

HOW TO USE THIS BOOK

Tᴴɪs book is divided into four seasonal sections, beginning with the Spring. Each section has a page of useful information about the season and includes the colours, flowers and festivals connected to the particular time of the year. Each season is then divided into monthly sections and a specially selected cake recipe is given at the start of each month. Detailed, step-by-step instructions then follow for appropriately decorated celebration cakes with instructions for making exquisite sugar flowers or for figure piping where these are required. The book commences with a section of basic recipes and instructions for making coverings, pastes and royal icing.

The book contains many designs which can be easily adapted for other occasions or times of year. For example, the lily cake illustrated for a Pearl Anniversary could also be an exotic Birthday cake for a special lady. The Leo Zodiac cake shown can be adapted to any sign by changing the central motif and piping Happy Birthday under the appropriate sign. When preparing a Zodiac cake it should be borne in mind that the sign does not start at the beginning of the month. This book has the Leo cake in the month of July as this month commences with Cancer and ends with Leo.

A list of Zodiac signs with the appropriate dates and symbol are given here for ease of reference as are Wedding Anniversaries.

Tʜᴇ Zᴏᴅɪᴀᴄ

♈	ARIES	*March 21 – April 20*	The Ram
♉	TAURUS	*April 21 – May 20*	The Bull
♊	GEMINI	*May 21 – June 21*	The Twins
♋	CANCER	*June 22 – July 23*	The Crab
♌	LEO	*July 24 – August 23*	The Lion
♍	VIRGO	*August 24 – September 23*	The Young Maiden
♎	LIBRA	*September 24 – October 22*	The Scales
♏	SCORPIO	*October 23 – November 22*	The Scorpion
♐	SAGITTARIUS	*November 23 – December 22*	The Centaur
♑	CAPRICORN	*December 23 – January 20*	The Goat
♒	AQUARIUS	*January 21 – February 19*	The Water Bearer
♓	PISCES	*February 20 – March 20*	The Fishes

Wᴇᴅᴅɪɴɢ Aɴɴɪᴠᴇʀsᴀʀɪᴇs

1st	*Cotton*	14th	*Ivory*
2nd	*Paper*	15th	*Crystal*
3rd	*Leather*	20th	*China*
4th	*Fruit & Flower*	25th	*Silver*
5th	*Wood*	30th	*Pearl*
6th	*Sugar*	35th	*Coral*
7th	*Wool*	40th	*Ruby*
8th	*Bronze & Pottery*	45th	*Sapphire*
9th	*Willow Pottery*	50th	*Gold*
10th	*Tin*	55th	*Emerald*
11th	*Steel*	60th	*Diamond*
12th	*Silk & Fine Linen*	65th	*Blue Sapphire*
13th	*Lace*	70th	*Platinum*

Basic recipes and instructions

ALMOND PASTE

Caster Sugar	170g (6oz)
Icing Sugar (sieved)	170g (6oz)
Ground Almonds	340g (12oz)
Glucose Syrup	225g (8oz)

Mix all dry ingredients together. Warm and pour in the glucose. Mix together to form a pliable paste. Store in sealed container until required.
NOTE: The consistency of the paste can be altered by adjusting the quantity of glucose.

ALBUMEN SOLUTION

Pure Albumen Powder	30g (1oz)
Water	170g (6oz)

Pour water into a bowl and stir whilst sprinkling in the dried albumen. Thoroughly mix and leave to stand for 1 hour. (Stir occasionally). Strain mixture through a sieve or muslin. Store in closed container in the refrigerator until required.

ROYAL ICING

Fresh Egg Whites or Albumen Solution	85g (3oz)
Icing Sugar (sieved)	455g (16oz)

Pour the albumen solution or fresh egg white into a bowl. Stir in one-third of the icing sugar and beat well. Continue beating in the icing sugar until all is used. Beat mixture until light, fluffy and peaks can be formed. Scrape inside of bowl and cover with a damp cloth. Use when required.
NOTE: Separate the egg whites 24 hours before use.

SOFT-CUTTING ROYAL ICING

Per 455g (16oz) of READY-MADE ROYAL ICING mix in:
1 Teaspoon of glycerine for the bottom tier of a 3-tier wedding cake.

2 Teaspoons of glycerine for the middle tier of a 3-tier or bottom tier of a 2-tier wedding cake.

3 Teaspoons for top tier, or single tier cakes.
NOTE: *Glycerine must only be added after the royal icing has been made.* **Do not** *add glycerine to royal icing for run-outs or No. 1 work.*

SUGARPASTE

Icing Sugar (sieved)	455g(16oz)
Egg White	1
Liquid Glucose (warmed)	60g (2oz)

Warm a bowl, containing the glucose, in a saucepan of hot water. Then add the egg white and warmed glucose to the icing sugar in a mixing bowl. Mix thoroughly. Knead the mixture to a pliable paste and then wrap it in a polythene bag. Store in a cool place until required.
NOTE: *Separate the egg white 24 hours before required.*

FLOWER PASTE

Cornflour	60g (2oz)
Icing Sugar (sieved)	400g (14oz)
Gum Tragacanth	22g (¾ oz)
Glucose Syrup	22g (¾ oz)
Cold Water	60g (2oz)
White Fat	22g (¾ oz)

Sieve the icing sugar, cornflour and gum tragacanth together. Then place into a mixing bowl. Add the remaining ingredients and thoroughly mix. The paste is properly mixed when it does not stick to the sides of the bowl. Mould the paste into a ball. Place in a polythene bag and leave to mature for at least 24 hours in a refrigerator. It is then ready for use.

BUTTERCREAM

Butter	115g(4oz)
Icing Sugar	170-225g(6-8oz)
Warm Water	1–2 Tablespoons
Essence or flavouring	To taste

Sieve the icing sugar. Soften butter and beat until light. Gradually add the icing sugar, beating well after each addition. Carefully add essence or flavouring of choice and water. Beat well. Store in refrigerator.

WEIGHING EGGS

NOTE: *The weight given for fresh eggs in the monthly cake recipes is that of eggs* **without shells**. *To weigh, break the eggs into a clean and grease-free bowl, stir together and weigh the amount required.*

GUM ARABIC SOLUTION

Boil 85g (3ozs) of water. Remove from heat and immediately whisk in 30g (1oz) of gum arabic powder. Leave to cool. Remove any surface film and store in a refrigerator until required.

NOTE: All ingredients should be at room temperature unless otherwise stated.

Spring

Spring is the time for the blossoming of new life and Mary's designs for celebration cakes for this season reflect the joy of nature and the glorious colours of spring flowers.

Lambs, bunnies and chicks have traditionally been popular decorations for Easter and Spring cakes, as have primroses, daffodils and violets. The imaginative cake-maker can however find new ways of presenting these old favourites, as Mary demonstrates with her enchanting Easter Duckling Cake.

The colour and design of a Spring celebration cake can be linked to the theme of colour: the pale greens of buds and new leaves, the soft yellows of primroses and daffodils, or the muted mauve of the violet. Spring colour can also be found in the delicate and appealing face of the pansy with its myriad colourful variations. For a stronger impact, a small amount of the vivid colouring of tulips and other bulbs can be used to enhance designs.

TRADITIONAL FLOWER OF THE MONTH

March   *Violet*
April   *Daisy*
May   *Hawthorn*

FESTIVALS

Easter
Mothering Sunday
Cup Final Day
St David's Day   *1st March*
Mother-in-law Day   *5th March*
St Patrick's Day   *17th March*
Primrose Day   *19th April*
Walpurgis Night   *30th April*
May Day (Beltane)   *1st May*
Washington's Birthday   *February*
Anzac Day   *25th April*
Victoria Day   *May*
Memorial Day   *May*

COLOUR OF THE MONTH

March   *Soft Sea-Green*
April   *Red*
May   *Pink*

·T·W·

March

Light Fruit Cake

INGREDIENTS

Butter	170g	(6oz)
Caster Sugar	170g	(6oz)
Ground Almonds	45g	(1½oz)
Fresh Egg	170g	(6oz)
Self Raising Flour	170g	(6oz)
Cherries (halved)	115g	(4oz)
Cherries (chopped)	60g	(2oz)
Currants	145g	(5oz)
Sultanas	170g	(6oz)
Mixed Peel	85g	(3oz)
Rum	30g	(1oz)
Lemon Zest & Juice		½ lemon

○ Approximate baking time 2 hours
○ Baking temperature 170°C (325°F)
or Gas Mark 3

TIN PREPARATION

Grease a 20.5cm (8") round tin with white fat and line it with greaseproof paper. Then grease the paper with white fat.

METHOD

Heat the oven to the recommended temperature.

Beat the butter and sugar until light and fluffy, then stir in the ground almonds. Lightly mix the eggs together in a separate bowl. Thoroughly beat in a small portion of egg at a time until all the egg is used. Carefully fold in the sieved flour to form a batter.

Mix all fruit, rum, lemon zest and juice together. Stir into the batter until evenly dispersed.

Spread mixture into the prepared tin. Bake in the centre of the oven.

After baking, leave the cake in the tin for thirty minutes. Then remove from tin onto a wire tray until cold. Wrap cake in waxed paper and leave to mature for three days.

Daffodil

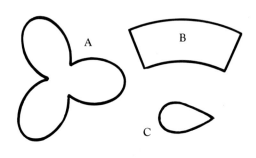

A metal or plastic cutter in each of the shapes shown is required. If a cutter is not available, the shape can be traced on to card and used as a template.

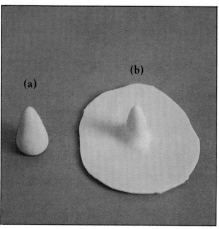

1 (**a**) *Form a cone from flower paste, then* (**b**) *thin out base of cone to create the shape shown.*

2 *Using cutter shape* **A**, *carefully cut out petal shape from* **1(b)** *keeping the cone protruding in the centre.*

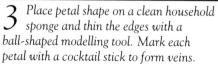

3 *Place petal shape on a clean household sponge and thin the edges with a ball-shaped modelling tool. Mark each petal with a cocktail stick to form veins.*

4 *Cut, and bend, a length of 24 gauge wire. Moisten hook with egg white and insert through the centre of the cone, until hidden.*

5 *Using cutter shape* **A**, *cut petal shape from thinly rolled flower paste. Place on household sponge and thin edges with a ball-shaped modelling tool. Vein and shape.*

6 Moisten centre of petal shape from step **4** and fix petal shape from step **5** into position shown. Leave to dry 24 hours.

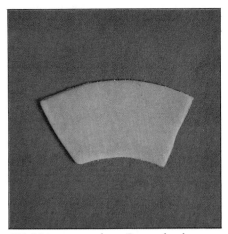

7 Using cutter shape **B**, cut the shape shown from thinly rolled flower paste.

8 Frill the outer edge by rolling a cocktail stick backwards and forwards a little at a time.

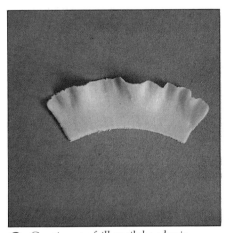

9 Continue to frill until the edge is completely frilled. Then cut to width shown.

10 Moisten one end and fix in place as shown, to form the flower's trumpet. Leave to dry 24 hours.

11 Moisten and fix trumpet in position. Fix three single stamens into centre of trumpet using a little yellow royal icing or flower paste.

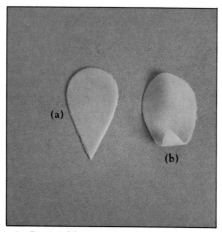

12 (a) *Using cutter shape C, cut a sepal from thinly rolled flower paste. Gently thin edge.* (b) *Curl end as shown to form sepal.*

13 *Moisten sepal and fix to base of daffodil as shown, ensure curled end is at top.*

14 *Form a cone from flower paste, with a hollowed out centre.*

15 *Moisten centre of cone and insert stem through it. Mould cone around flower base and sepal. Wrap floral tape around the stem.*

16 *Using a clean, fine artists' brush, tint the flower and back of the sepal with confectioners' dusting powder.*

17 *Picture shows a bloom with trumpet made from orange coloured paste.*

Mother's Day

TEMPLATE

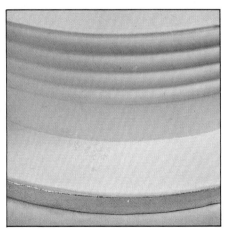

1 Coat a cake and board with royal icing (using a patterned scraper to create the fluted design on the cake-side as shown).

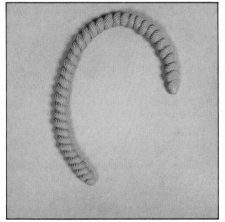

2 Using the template as a guide, pipe a rope on waxed paper to form the basket handle (No. 43). Leave to dry 24 hours.

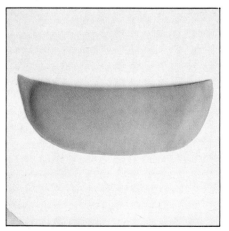

3 Transfer the basket-side template to thin card. Place on thinly rolled sugar paste and cut round it. Fix the basket-side to the cake-top.

4 Using the template as a guide, pipe a line above the basket (No. 1). Then cover the top space with filigree (No. 0).

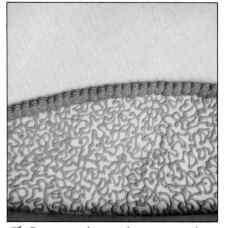

5 Pipe a rope line on the top outer edge of the basket (No. 43).

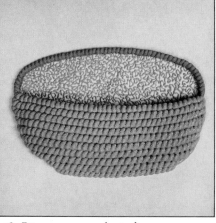

6 Pipe neat rows of rope lines to complete the basket (No. 43).

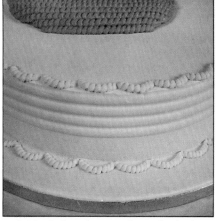

7 Mark the cake-top edge and cake-base into 32 sections. Then pipe a curved rope line in each section (No. 43).

8 Pipe a frill against each curved rope line (No. 57). Then pipe graduated dots around cake-base (No. 2).

9 Make and fix daffodils (see pages 10-12) and leaves to the basket as shown.

10 Fix the basket handle in position. Leave to dry 2 hours, then make and fix ribbon bows.

11 *Pipe inscription of choice below the basket (No. 1). Then pipe tracery around the inscription (No. 1). Fix artificial butterfly as shown.*

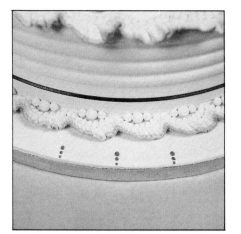

12 *Pipe graduated dots around the cake board edge opposite each indentation (No. 1).*

April

Simnel Cake

Ingredients

Butter	225g	(8oz)
Soft Brown Sugar	225g	(8oz)
Fresh Egg	225g	(8oz)
Plain Flour	285g	(10oz)
Ground Cinnamon	½	Teaspoon
Ground Nutmeg	½	Teaspoon
Cocoa Powder	3	Teaspoons
Currants	455g	(16oz)
Sultanas	145g	(5oz)
Ground Almonds	85g	(3oz)
Almond Paste	170g	(6oz)

○ Approximate baking time 2½ hours
○ Baking temperature 170°C (325°F)
or Gas Mark 3

Tin Preparation

Grease a 20.5cm (8″) round tin with white fat and line it with greaseproof paper. Then grease the paper with white fat.

Method

Heat the oven to the recommended temperature.

Roll the almond paste into an 18cm (7″) circle.

Sieve together the flour, spices and cocoa powder.

Cream the fat and sugar until light and fluffy.

Lightly mix the egg in a separate bowl. Thoroughly beat a small portion of the egg a little at a time into the creamed fat and sugar until all the egg is used.

Carefully fold the sieved flour, spices and cocoa powder into the batter. Stir in the fruit and ground almonds.

Spread half the mixture into the prepared cake tin. Place the circle of almond paste on top.

Spread the remainder of the mixture over the almond paste.

Bake in the centre of the oven.

After baking leave the cake in the tin for thirty minutes and then remove on to a wire tray until cold. Wrap in waxed paper and allow to mature for one week.

The cake can be decorated following the instructions on pages 20-21.

Easter Ducklings

TEMPLATE

1 Cut five-petal flower shapes from thinly rolled sugar-paste. Indent centres. Pipe-in royal icing stamens (No. 1). Make sugarpaste leaves (see picture 10). Leave to dry 24 hours.

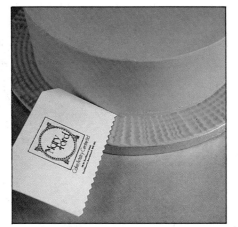

2 Coat a cake and board with royal icing (using a comb scraper to create the fluted design on the board as shown).

3 Pipe long leaves against cake-side, using a piping bag cut to a 'V' shape at tip.

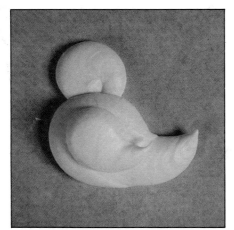

4 Trace templates on to card. Cover with waxed paper and pipe-in ducks following direction of arrows, using royal icing without glycerine (No. 4). Make 2 large and 20 small.

5 Leave ducks to dry 24 hours. Remove large ducks from waxed paper and reverse. Pipe the matching design on the backs. Leave to dry 24 hours. Pipe beak and eyes (No. 1).

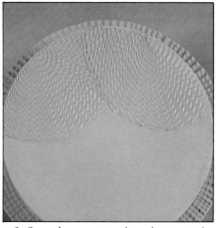

6 *Spread a quantity of royal icing on the cake-top and immediately create the ripple effect by using the comb scraper from step 2.*

7 *Fix flowers, leaves and large ducks to the rippled area.*

8 *Pipe a border of leaves along the facing edge of the rippled design (No. 1).*

9 *Pipe inscription of choice (No. 2). Then overpipe inscription (No. 1). Decorate with wavy lines (No. 1).*

10 *Pipe scrolls on cake-top along the rippled edge (No. 43).*

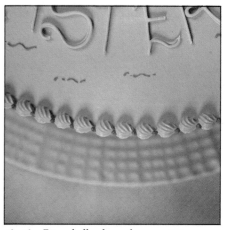

11 *Pipe shells along the remaining cake-top edge (No. 43).*

12 To decorate the cake board, fix groups of small ducks in position as shown.

13 Fix sugarpaste flowers between the groups of ducks to complete the cake decoration.

Simnel Cake

1 Glaze a cold simnel cake-top with boiled apricot purée. Make and fix almond paste crimped balls. Place on a baking tray. Leave to dry 24 hours.

2 Place the cake under the grill or in a very hot oven to colour the almond paste as shown. Immediately glaze the cake-top and almond paste with gum arabic solution.

3 Warm readymade fondant in a saucepan over hot water until it reaches 38°C (100°F).

4 Immediately pour the warmed fondant on to the cake-top. Leave to set for 2 hours.

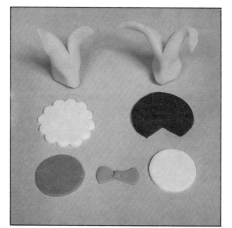

5 Cut, mould and shape all the pieces shown from marzipan or sugarpaste. Leave to dry 2 hours.

6 Fix the pieces together and decorate to make rabbit-tops (No. 1).

7 Fix the rabbits to the cake-top in the position shown.

8 Pipe, and decorate with tracery, the inscription of choice on the cake-top, using royal icing (No. 1). Fix cake frill around the cake-side.

Apple Blossom

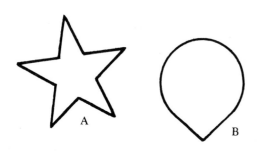

A metal or plastic cutter in each of the shapes shown is required. If a cutter is not available, the shape can be traced on to card and used as a template.

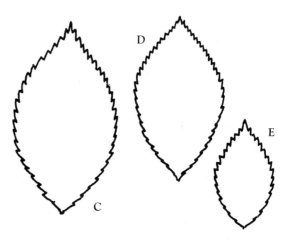

MAKING A BUD

1 Cut and bend, a length of 28 gauge wire. Mould flower paste into a ball and insert moistened wire. Mark five petals. Leave to dry 24 hours.

*2 Using cutter shape **A**, cut out calyx from thinly rolled flower paste.*

3 Moisten calyx and insert wire through centre then wrap it around the bud, as shown. Leave to dry 24 hours.

4 Using a clean, soft paintbrush, tint with confectioners' dusting powder to complete the bud.

MAKING A CALYX

5 Form a cone from flower paste.
Gently flatten the base out leaving top
of cone protruding as shown.

6 Using a cutter in the shape of **A**
carefully cut a calyx from the moulded
flower paste.

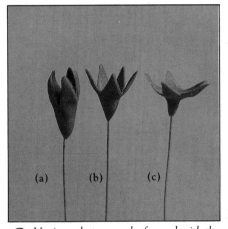

7 Bend a length of 24 gauge wire to
form hook. Moisten with egg white,
then carefully insert through centre of
calyx until the hook is hidden.

8 Various shapes can be formed with the
calyx. (**a**) is for a half open bud, (**b**)
a half open blossom, and (**c**) a full bloom.

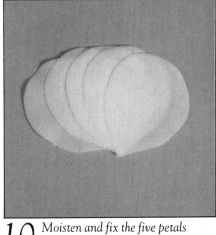

MAKING A HALF OPEN BUD

9 With cutter shape **B**, cut five petals
from thinly rolled flower paste.

10 Moisten and fix the five petals
together, overlapping as shown.

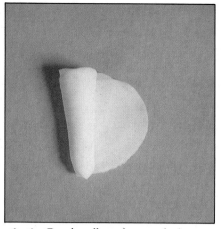

11 Gently roll petals towards the centre as shown, keeping a hollow centre.

12 Moisten end of petal then continue rolling until the petals form the completed tube shape.

13 Moisten base of tube and insert into calyx shape (**b**) (see step **8**). Leave to dry 24 hours. Tint edges of petals with confectioners' dusting powder.

MAKING HALF OPEN BLOSSOM

14 Using cutter shape **B**, cut petal from flower paste. Place petal on household sponge and flatten edges.

15 Moisten base of petal and fix to centre of calyx shape (**b**) (see step **8**).

16 Repeat step **14** to form another petal. Moisten and insert into calyx, overlapping the first petal as shown.

17 Repeat step **14** three times more, until five petals have been fixed into place. Insert five stamens into the flower centre. Leave to dry 24 hours.

18 Using a clean, fine, soft artists' brush, tint petals with confectioners' dusting powder.

MAKING A FULL BLOOM
19 Repeat steps **14-16**, using calyx (**c**) (see step **8**) and keeping the petals well spread.

20 Repeat step **14** three times more, until 5 petals have been fixed into place. Insert five stamens into the flower centre. Leave to dry 24 hours.

21 A calyx can also be used without petals, as shown, for a fallen bloom. Leave to dry 24 hours before tinting the centre with lustre colour.

22 Make a spray using the various stages in the life cycle of the apple blossom. Make leaves using cutter shapes **C**, **D** and **E** (follow instructions on page 43).

Aimee

TEMPLATE

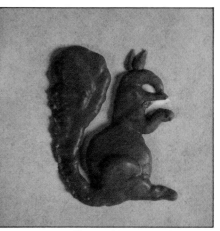

1 *Trace small squirrel template onto card and cover with waxed paper. Pipe-in squirrel as shown (use royal icing without glycerine), then leave to dry 24 hours.*

2 *Trace large squirrel template onto card and cover with waxed paper. Pipe-in tail, ears and acorn top. Leave to dry 1 hour.*

3 *Pipe-in body and acorn cup. Brush-in eye with icing. Leave to dry 24 hours, then paint eye with edible food colouring.*

4 *Make (using instructions from pages 22-25) and fix apple blossom branch on cake-top in the position shown.*

5 *Fix a squirrel of each size to apple blossom branch as shown.*

6 *Pipe inscription of choice on cake-top (No. 1). Then overpipe inscription (No. 1). Pipe delicate tracery around inscription (No. 0).*

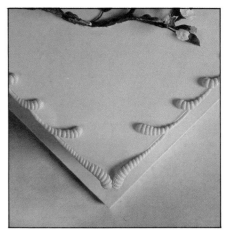

7 *Pipe scrolls along the back cake-top edge on two sides of the cake (No. 43).*

8 *Pipe bulbs along remaining two sides of the cake-top edge, and then along each cake-base side (No. 3).*

9 *Pipe a line beside the cake-top scrolls, finishing with a spiral at each end as shown (No. 2).*

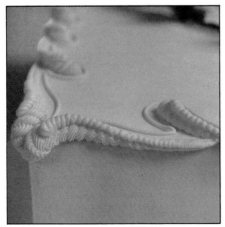

10 *Overpipe each cake-top scroll (No. 2).*

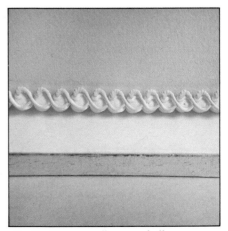

11 *Pipe a scroll on two bulbs at cake-base (No. 2). Overpipe each cake-base scroll as shown (No. 1).*

12 Overpipe each cake-top scroll (No. 1).

13 Fix to each corner of cake board a spray of apple blossom, leaves and buds. Fix ribbon around cake board edge.

May

Coffee and walnut cake

Ingredients

Margarine	170g	(6oz)
Caster Sugar	170g	(6oz)
Plain flour	225g	(8oz)
Baking powder	1½ Teaspoons	
Milk	2 Tablespoons	
Fresh eggs	170g	(6oz)
Instant coffee powder	2 Teaspoons	
Walnuts (chopped)	85g	(3oz)
(for decoration)	45g (1½oz)	

○ Approximate baking time 40 minutes
○ Baking temperature 170°C (325°F)
        or Gas Mark 3

Tin preparation

Grease the inside of a 20.5cm (8″) round tin with white fat and line it with greaseproof paper. Then grease the paper with white fat.

Method

Heat the oven to the recommended temperature.
Sieve together the flour, baking powder and coffee powder.
Beat the margarine and sugar until light and fluffy.
Lightly mix the eggs and milk together in a separate bowl. Thoroughly beat in the liquid a little at a time.
Carefully fold the sieved ingredients into the batter. Stir in the chopped walnuts.
Transfer the mixture to the tin and spread evenly. Then place walnuts over the mixture and bake.
After baking, leave the cake in the tin for thirty minutes. Then remove from the tin and place on to a wire tray until cold. Use within three days of baking.

Pansy

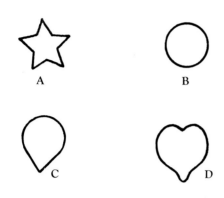

A B

C D

A metal or plastic cutter in each of the shapes shown is required. If a cutter is not available, the shape can be traced on to card and used as a template.

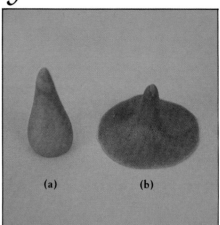

(a) (b)

1 (a) Form a cone from flower paste, then (b) thin out the base of the cone to create the shape shown.

2 Using cutter shape A, carefully cut out a calyx from step 1(b).

3 Cut and bend a length of 24 gauge wire. Moisten hook with egg white and insert into side of calyx, then shape as shown. Leave to dry 24 hours.

4 Using cutter shape B, cut a petal from thinly rolled flower paste.

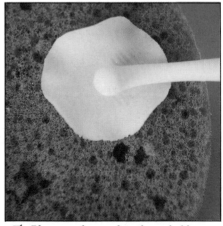

5 Place petal on a clean household sponge, then gently thin and shape using a ball-shaped modelling tool.

6 Moisten petal and fix to top of calyx. Repeat steps **4-5** and fix second petal to top of calyx, overlapping as shown.

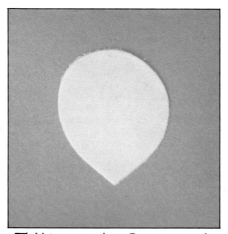

7 Using cutter shape **C**, cut two petals from thinly rolled flower paste. Repeat step **5** for each petal.

8 Moisten and fix one petal below and to the right of the top petals. Then fix other petal to the opposite side.

9 Using cutter shape **D**, cut the bottom petal from thinly rolled flower paste.

10 Moisten and fix to bottom half of calyx. Make the hollow centre of the flower, using a cocktail stick. Leave to dry 24 hours.

11 Using a fine, clean, soft artists' brush, colour the blooms with a variety of edible food colours and confectioners' dusting powders.

Celebration

**TEMPLATE FOR
20.5CM (8") ROUND CAKE**

1 Using the instructions for making pansies on pages 30-31, make a posy as shown.

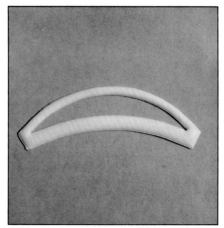

2 Using the template as a guide, outline crescent shape on waxed paper with royal icing (No. 1) and then flood-in. Leave to dry 24 hours. 12 runouts are required.

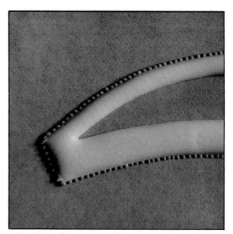

3 Pipe dots around the outer edge of each runout (No. 0). Leave to dry 2 hours.

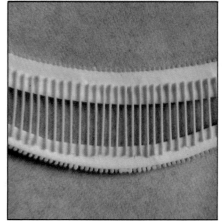

4 Carefully remove each runout from the waxed paper. Turn the runout over and then pipe lines across the centre (No. 0). Leave to dry 24 hours.

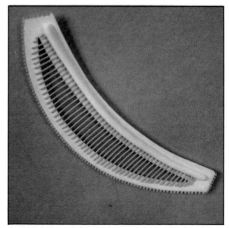

5 Pipe a thick line on six runouts (No. 2) on the inner part as shown. Leave to dry 12 hours. (For cake-base.)

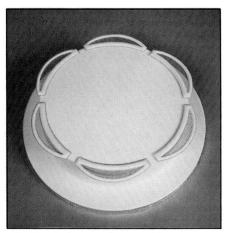

6 Fix six decorated runout pieces around the cake-top edge in the position shown.

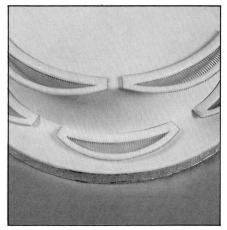

7 Fix the decorated runouts (with piped line) around cake-base as shown. Leave to dry 2 hours.

8 Pipe bulbs on each case base runout as shown (No. 1).

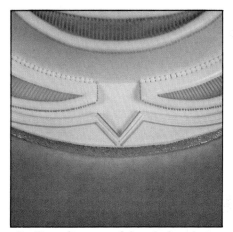

9 Pipe a line around the cake board (No. 2). Pipe a line beside the No. 2 line. Then overpipe the No. 2 line (No. 1).

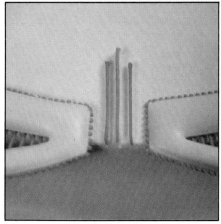

10 Pipe parallel lines between each cake-top runout as shown (No. 2 and 1).

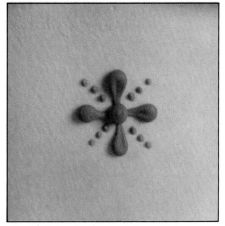

11 Pipe the decorative motif shown around the centre of the cake-side (No. 1).

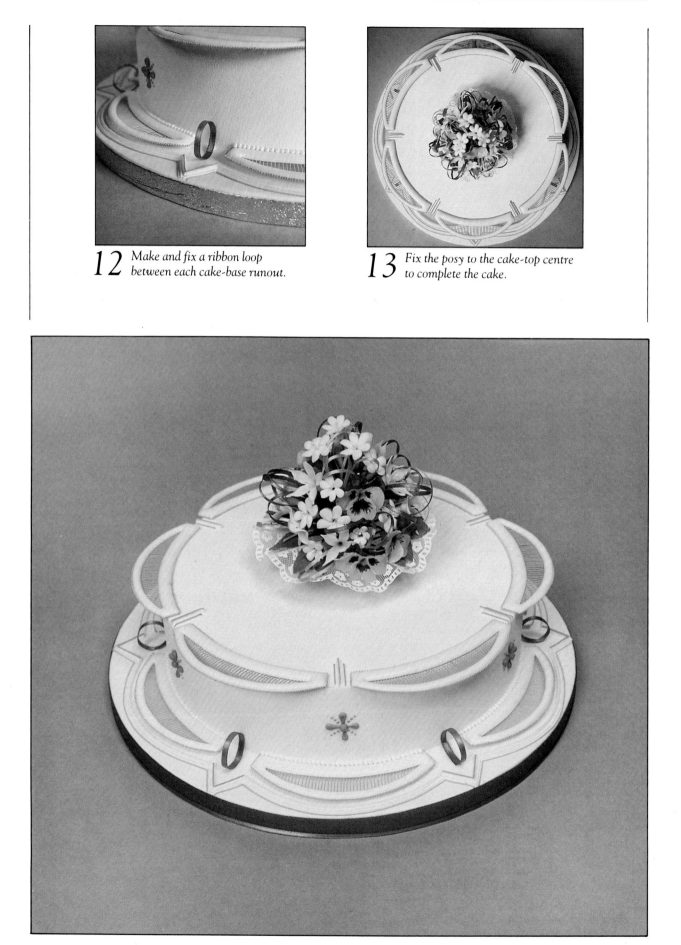

12 Make and fix a ribbon loop between each cake-base runout.

13 Fix the posy to the cake-top centre to complete the cake.

Zara

1 Cut out semi-circles of thinly rolled sugarpaste with a crimped cutter. Fix into place on the top-edge of a coated cake and board.

2 Make sugarpaste shapes as shown to form body, head and hat.

3 Fix pieces together and decorate as shown (No. 1). 16 figures are required.

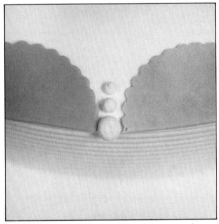

4 Pipe graduated bulbs between each semi-circle (No. 2).

5 Fix a crimped circle of sugarpaste to cake-top centre. Fix a stick of rock to the centre and decorate base with artificial flowers.

6 Pipe shells (No. 5), dots and lines (No. 1) around Maypole-base as shown.

7 Fix bodies to the centre of each crimped semi-circle.

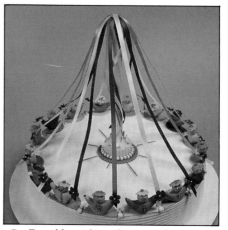

8 Fix ribbons from the top of the Maypole to the left hand of each body using a small flower.

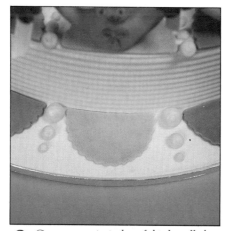

9 Cut out semi-circles of thinly rolled sugarpaste with a crimped cutter and fix to cake board as shown. Pipe graduated dots between each semi-circle (No. 2).

10 Make ribbon loops and attach to each semi-circle around cake-base.

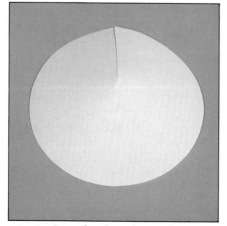

11 Cut a disc from thin card. Cut a straight line to the centre and form into a cone. Fix in place.

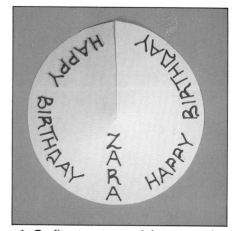

12 Pipe inscription of choice around the cone-edge (No. 1). Leave to dry 1 hour.

13 Carefully fix the cone to the top of the Maypole and decorate centre with ribbon loops.

14 Pipe loops around the cone-edge and a dot at each loop-join (No. 1).

Summer

IN SUMMER the cake decorator has a wonderful choice of flower colours to inspire the imagination, and many opportunities to bake cakes for afternoon tea or picnics.

Roses, which bloom throughout the summer, are the most popular flower for wedding cakes and can be linked into an overall colour scheme or match the bridal bouquet. This versatile flower can, however, be used to enhance many different occasions, as Mary shows in her thoughtful cake for a fortunate lady.

The delicate summer colours harmonise beautifully with floral artistry, as in Mary's gentle Scabius Wedding Cake. The more riotous colours of the summer blooms should be used sparingly on cakes as otherwise they become overwhelming. However, used creatively these colours can have a dramatic effect on a cake for a special occasion.

TRADITIONAL FLOWER OF THE MONTH

June   *Honeysuckle*
July   *Water Lily*
August   *Poppy*

FESTIVALS

Father's Day
Alexandra Rose Day   *June*
Summer Solstice   *21st June*
Midsummer Day   *24th June*
Orange Day   *12th July*
Canada Day   *July*
Independence Day   *4th July*
Australia Day   *26th July*

COLOUR OF THE MONTH

June   *Lemon Yellow*
July   *Green*
August   *Golden Yellow*

·T·W·

June

Sponge Cake

INGREDIENTS

Fresh Egg	85g	(3oz)
Caster Sugar	85g	(3oz)
Self Raising Flour (sieved)	85g	(3oz)
Hot Water	1½ Teaspoons	

○ Approximate baking time 14 minutes
○ Baking temperature 200°C (400°F) or Gas Mark 6

TIN PREPARATION

Grease a 20.5cm (8″) round sponge tin with white fat, and then sprinkle sufficient flour into the tin to cover the inside. Gently shake the tin to ensure the fat is covered, then tap out any excess.

METHOD

Heat the oven to the recommended temperature.
Lightly whisk the egg in a bowl.
Pour in the caster sugar and whisk briskly until light and creamy.
Stir in the hot water.
Gently fold in the sieved flour with a spatula.
Transfer the mixture to the tin.
Bake the sponge near the top of the preheated oven.
After baking, leave the sponge in the tin for five minutes. Then remove from tin on to a greaseproof paper covered in caster sugar, upturn the sponge and place on to a wire tray until cold.
Wrap sponge in waxed paper and store in deep-freeze for up to six months. Use within three days of baking or after defrosting.

Hybrid Rose

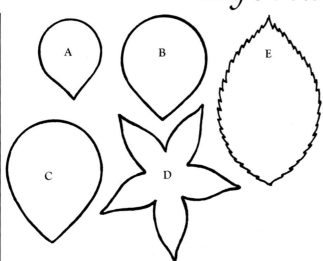

A metal or plastic cutter in each of the shapes shown is required. If a cutter is not available, the shape can be traced on to card and used as a template.

1 Cut and bend a length of lime green 24 gauge wire.

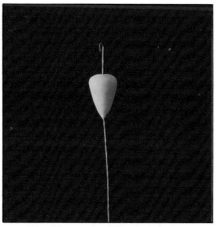

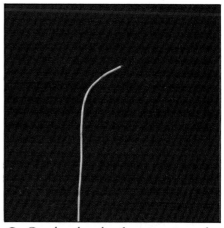

2 Mould a piece of flower paste into a cone. Moisten hook end of wire and insert into cone. Pull wire through cone until the hook is hidden. This forms the flower head.

3 Cut short lengths of stamen wire and bend to shape shown.

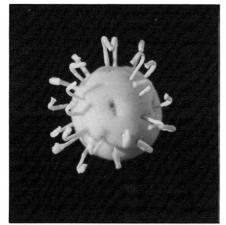

4 Insert each length of stamen wire around the parameter of the flower head.

5 Moisten a stamen wire with egg white and sprinkle coloured rice flour onto it. The 'pollen' should stick quite thickly. Test for colour strength.

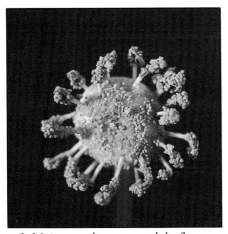

6 *Moisten each stamen and the flower centre, then immediately cover with coloured rice flour to give the pollen effect shown. Leave to dry 24 hours.*

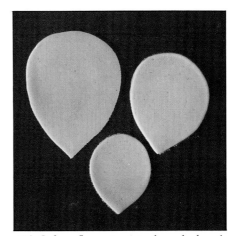

7 *Colour flower paste to three shades of basic colour required. Use the deepest colour for inside petals, medium for middle and lightest for outer petals.*

8 *Cut and place an **A** size petal on a clean household sponge. Thin the edge with a ball-shaped modelling tool.*

9 *Moisten base of petal and fix to flower centre. Fix four more **A** size petals, overlapping as necessary.*

10 *Gently ease the petals into the shape shown using the side of the finger.*

11 *Cut, shape and fix eight **B** size petals. Allow to dry for 30 minutes.*

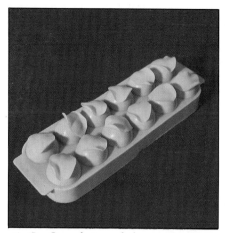

12 Cut, shape and place twelve **C** size petals on to a curved surface. (This gives two spare petals). Leave to dry 1 hour.

13 Moisten and fix ten petals to the back of the flower, overlapping as shown.

14 Turn rose to the front and check that the shape is even.

15 Roll out two pieces of flower paste – one white, one green – and fix together. Using cutter shape **D**, cut out a calyx.

16 Moisten calyx and insert wire through centre. Fix and shape the calyx to back of rose.

17 Mould a cone shape, insert wire through it, and then fix to calyx as shown. Leave to dry 24 hours.

18 *Delicately tint the rose petals, using a fine, soft artists' brush, with confectioners' dusting powder.*

19 *A rosebud can be formed using petal shapes **B** and **C**, and calyx shape **D**.*

20 *Using cutter shape **E**, cut a leaf from thinly rolled flower paste – keep the base slightly thicker.*

21 *Press the leaf onto a veiner then peel it off gently, or mark the leaf with a cocktail stick, to form veins.*

22 *Cut a length of 26 gauge wire, moisten one end and insert into leaf. Colour and then varnish the leaf with edible confectioners' varnish.*

23 *A spray can be formed using five leaves, one rosebud and one open bloom, bound together with floral tape.*

Rosanna

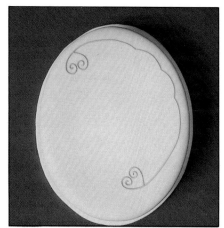

1 Pipe curved lines and heart motifs, using royal icing (No. 1) on an oval shaped, sugarpaste coated cake as shown.

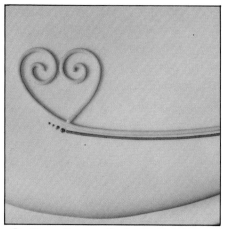

2 Pipe a line outside the first line (No. 1). Finish line with small dots as shown.

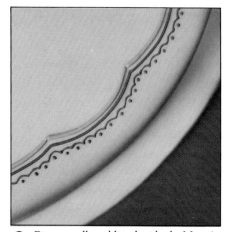

3 Pipe a scalloped line beside the No. 1 line (No. 0). Then pipe a dot inside each scallop (No. 0).

4 Fix rose spray to cake-top in position shown. Pipe inscription of choice (No. 1).

5 Decorate inscription with piped scrolls, under each capital letter and tracery, as shown (No. 0).

6 Pipe plain shells around the cake-base (No. 3).

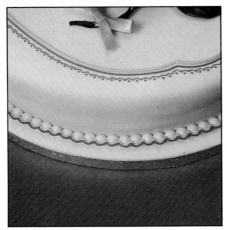

7 *Pipe a line over each shell (No. 2). Then overpipe the No. 2 line (No. 1).*

8 *Pipe a scalloped line around the cake board edge (No. 0). Then pipe a dot inside each scallop (No. 0).*

Father's Day

TEMPLATES

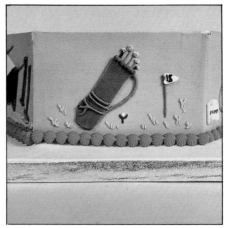

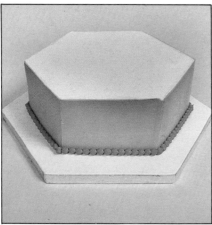

1 Coat an hexagonal shaped cake and board with two colours of royal icing. Pipe shells around the cake-base (No. 43).

2 Using the template as a guide, cut golf scene from thinly rolled sugarpaste. Fix into place and decorate as shown (No. 1).

3 Using the template as a guide, cut, fix and decorate the artist's equipment.

4 Using the template as a guide, cut, fix and decorate the garden scene.

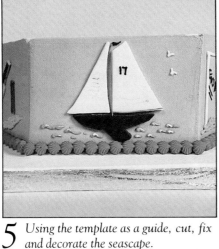

5 Using the template as a guide, cut, fix and decorate the seascape.

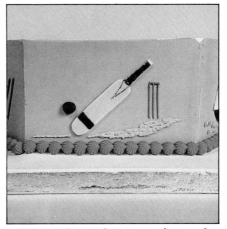

6 Using the template as a guide, cut, fix and decorate the cricket scene.

7 Using the template as a guide, cut, fix and decorate the football scene as shown.

8 Pipe shells around the cake-top edge (No. 43).

9 Using sugarpaste, make, fix and decorate several books to the cake-top as shown.

10 Pipe inscription of choice below the books and decorate with tracery (No. 1).

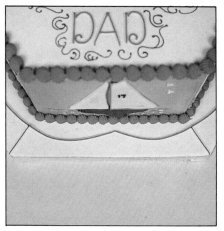

11 Pipe a curved line on the cake board, and pipe a straight line from the line to the cake board edge (No. 2). Overpipe the No. 2 lines (No. 1).

12 Pipe a line beside the overpiped line as shown (No. 1). Decorate the cake board edge with ribbon.

July

Cherry and Almond Cake

INGREDIENTS

Glacé Cherries (chopped)	255g	(9oz)
Self Raising Flour	285g	(10oz)
Salt	Pinch	
Butter	170g	(6oz)
Caster Sugar	170g	(6oz)
Eggs	255g	(9oz)
Ground Almonds	45g	(1½oz)

○ Baking time 1 hour
○ Baking temperature 170°C (325°F)
or Gas Mark 3

TIN PREPARATION

Grease an 20.5cm (8″) round sponge tin with white fat and line it with greaseproof paper. Then grease the paper with white fat.

METHOD

Heat the oven to the recommended temperature.
Wash and dry the cherries, then toss in a little flour and roughly chop.
Thoroughly sieve flour and salt together. Beat butter and sugar together until light and fluffy. Thoroughly beat the eggs into the mixture a little at a time with a tablespoon of flour.
Stir in the almonds, cherries and the remaining flour.
Spread the mixture into the prepared tin. Bake in the centre of the oven.
After baking leave the cake in the tin for five minutes. Remove from tin on to a wire tray until cold. Use within three days of baking.

Teddy Bears' Picnic

1 Coat a cake and board with royal icing (use a patterned scraper to create the side effect shown). Stipple the board with a fine sponge. Leave to dry 24 hours.

2 Cut an oval tablecloth from a thinly rolled sheet of sugarpaste. Frill edge by rolling a cocktail stick backwards and forwards. Decorate with piped flowers (No. 1).

3 Using sugarpaste form the various parts of a Teddy Bear shown. 6 Teddy Bears are required.

4 Assemble the Teddy Bears and decorate (No. 1). Make and decorate a honey pot.

5 Pipe rosettes around the cake-top edge and base (No. 42).

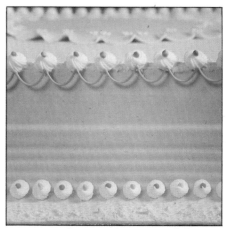

6 Pipe a dot on each rosette and then pipe a loop between each top rosette in alternate colours (No. 1).

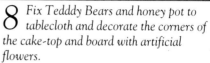

7 Pipe inscription of choice on cake-top and decorate with piped flowers (No. 1).

8 Fix Teddy Bears and honey pot to tablecloth and decorate the corners of the cake-top and board with artificial flowers.

Dave

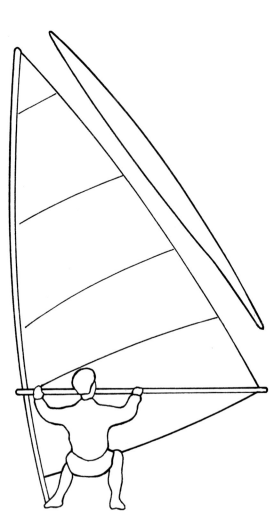

DAVE'S TEMPLATE

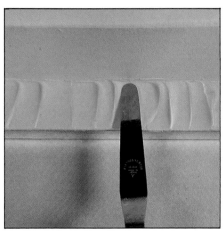

1 Coat a square cake with royal icing in the normal way. Using a palette knife, spread icing on the cake board to create waves.

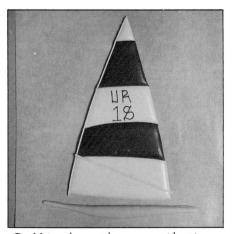

2 Using the templates as a guide, pipe royal icing outlines of the sail and board onto waxed paper (No. 1). Flood-in, then leave to dry 24 hours. Decorate as shown (No. 1).

3 Outline (No. 1) and flood-in the sailboard-rider on waxed paper. Leave to dry 24 hours. Decorate as shown (No. 1).

4 Carefully remove sail, sailboard and rider from waxed paper and fix to cake-top. Spread royal icing from sailboard to cake-corner to represent waves.

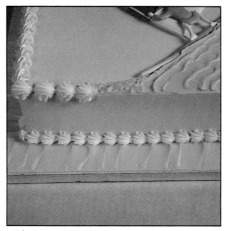

5 Pipe shells (using two colours of royal icing in the piping bag) around remaining cake-top edge and cake-base (No. 7).

6 Pipe inscription of choice on cake-top (No. 1). Decorate with keys if appropriate.

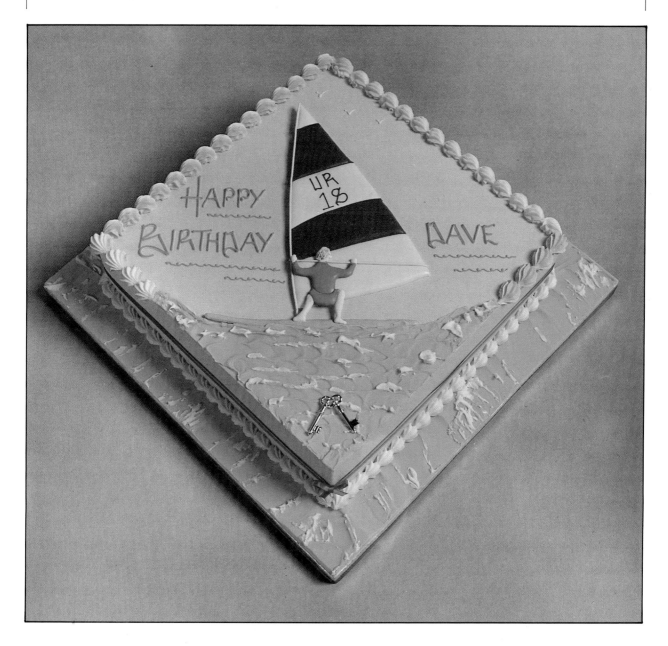

Leo

LEO'S TEMPLATE

1 Coat a 20.5cm (8") round cake and place on a 30.5cm (12") shaped board. (Use a comb-scraper on the cake-side). Flood-in the cake board. Leave to dry 24 hours.

2 Trace Leo's template on to card. Place waxed paper over the template and pipe the lines using royal icing without glycerine (No. 1).

3 Flood-in the head and body. Leave to dry 24 hours. Paint features with edible food colouring.

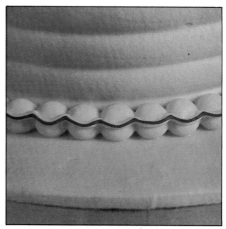

4 Divide the cake-top into 12 sections and pipe straight lines to the cake-centre. Pipe signs of zodiac around the cake-edge in piped boxes.

5 Pipe shells around the cake-base (No. 2). Then pipe a line on each shell (No. 1).

6 Pipe the names of the signs of the zodiac on the cake board (beneath the appropriate sign). Pipe 'Happy Birthday' under Leo (No. 1).

7 Carefully remove Leo from the waxed paper and fix into place in the cake-centre.

August

Passion Cake

INGREDIENTS

Plain Flour	225g	(8oz)
Bicarbonate of Soda	¾ Teaspoon	
Baking Powder	1½ Teaspoons	
Salt	½ Teaspoon	
Soft Light Brown Sugar	145g	(5oz)
Chopped Walnuts	45g	(1½oz)
Eggs	225g	(8oz)
Ripe Bananas	2	
Grated Carrots	145g	(5oz)
Oil	145g	(5oz)

○ Approximate baking time 1 hour

○ Baking temperature 180°C (350°F)
   or Gas Mark 4

TIN PREPARATION

Grease a 20.5cm (8″) round tin with white fat, and line it with greaseproof paper. Then grease the paper with white fat.

METHOD

Heat the oven to the recommended temperature.

Sieve the flour, bicarbonate of soda, baking powder and salt into a medium-sized mixing bowl. Add the brown sugar, chopped walnuts and beaten egg.

Peel and mash the bananas and add to the bowl, then add the grated carrots and oil. Mix in with a wooden spoon, and then beat well for one minute.

Put the mixture into the prepared tin. Bake in the centre of the oven.

After baking, leave the cake in the tin for five minutes. Then remove the cake from the tin and place onto a wire tray until cold.

Dust the top with icing sugar. Use within three days of making.

Scabius

A metal or plastic cutter in each of the shapes shown is required. If a cutter is not available, the shape can be traced on to card and used as a template.

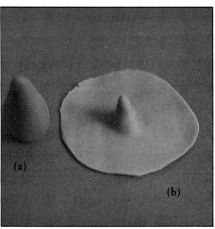

1 (a) Form a cone from flower paste, then (b) thin out the base of the cone to create the shape shown.

2 Using cutter shape C, carefully cut a calyx from step 1(b).

3 Place the calyx on a clean household sponge and gently thin and curl the edges up using a ball-shaped modelling tool.

4 Cut and bend a length of 24 gauge wire. Moisten hook with egg white and insert into cone as shown. Leave to dry 24 hours.

5 Using cutter shape A, cut a circle of petals from thinly rolled flower paste.

6 Carefully cut each projecting petal into two and separate slightly to form pairs of petals.

7 Frill each petal edge by rolling a cocktail stick backwards and forwards a little at a time.

8 Continue frilling the edge until it is well frilled all round.

9 Moisten back of petal and fix to the top of the calyx.

10 Using cutter shape **A**, repeat steps *5-8* to form another circle of petals. Moisten and fix to first.

11 Using cutter shape **B**, repeat steps *5-8* to form another circle of petals. Moisten and fix to second.

12 Form a cone from a very small piece of flower paste.

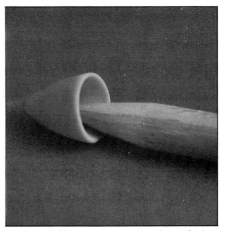

13 Hollow out cone using the end of a cocktail stick.

14 Make plenty of small hollow cones. Leave to dry 1 hour.

15 Moisten centre of flower and insert cones around inner petal edge as shown.

16 Insert sufficient cones to complete the flower centre. Leave to dry 24 hours.

17 Using a clean, fine and soft artists' brush, delicately tint the petals with confectioners' dusting powder.

Summer Wedding

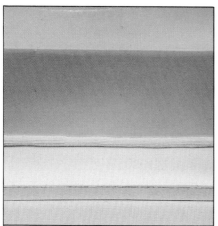

1 On a coated cake and board pipe a line along each side of the cake-base, using royal icing (No. 44).

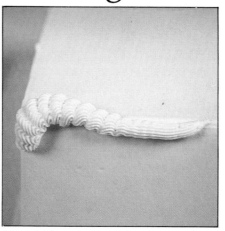

2 Divide each side of the cake-top edge into four. Pipe a left hand 'S' scroll on one corner as shown (No. 44).

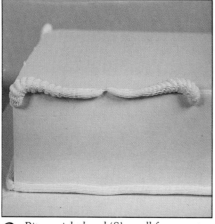

3 Pipe a right hand 'S' scroll from centre edge to meet first scroll.

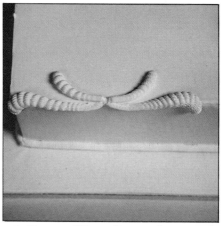

4 Pipe two 'C' scrolls towards centre of the 'S' scrolls, as shown.

5 Repeat steps **2-4** around the remaining cake-top edge. Pipe left and right hand scrolls around cake-base.

6 Overpipe each scroll around cake-top edge and base (No. 3).

7 Overpipe each scroll around cake-top edge and base (No. 2).

8 Tilt the cake and support, then pipe curved lines on each cake-side, in the pattern shown (No. 2).

9 Pipe beneath each curved line (No. 1). Then pipe a line against the No. 2 line (No. 1).

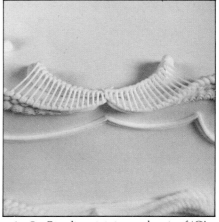

10 Pipe lines joining each pair of 'C' and 'S' scrolls to form a lattice (No. 1).

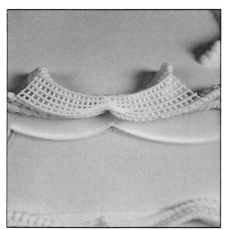

11 Pipe lines over the length of lattice (No. 1), starting from the wide gap and joining at the centre.

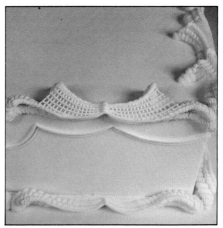

12 Overpipe each cake-top scroll (No. 1). Then pipe dots on each lattice centre (No. 1).

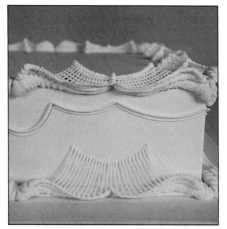

13 Pipe vertical lines from the cake-side to the base scrolls, as shown (No. 1).

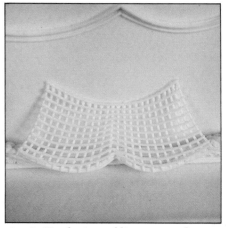

14 Pipe horizontal lines to complete the cake-side lattice (No. 1).

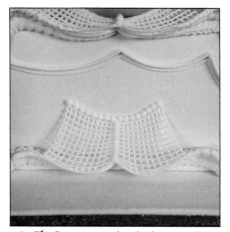

15 Overpipe each cake-base scroll (No. 1). Then pipe plain shells along the cake-side lattice edge (No. 1).

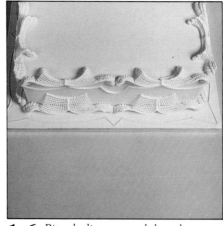

16 Pipe the lines around the cake board, as indicated (No. 2).

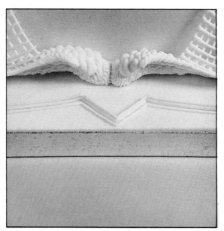

17 Pipe a line beside the cakeboard No. 2 line (No. 1). Then overpipe the No. 2 line (No. 1).

18 Fix a Scabius (from pages 57-59), ribbon loop and fill-in flowers to each cake-side corner and the centre of the bottom tier cake-top.

19 Fix a horseshoe at the centre of each cake board side with a piped dot (No. 0). Pipe a scallop line (No. 0) beside each cake board centre 'V' as shown.

20 Make a floral spray of scabius (from pages 57-59), fill-in flowers and ribbons to fill a vase for the cake-top.

Autumn

Autumn is the season of mellow fruitfulness and the celebration of the harvest safely gathered in. Mary was inspired by the simple beauty of wild fruits in the hedgerow to create her unusual blackberry cake to grace a seasonal celebration. Autumn colours can be both subtle and vibrant with rich shades of purple and red, or earthy browns fading through orange to golden tones and palest yellows; giving wide scope for the imaginative use of colour and texture. The chrysanthemum is the ideal flower for decorating celebration cakes for this season as it is to be found in all the subtle and glowing colours of autumn.

The autumn festivals offer an opportunity for the cake-maker to bake new recipes and designs appropriate to the occasion, such as deliciously different cakes to enjoy around the bonfire or a suitably scary Halloween party cake.

TRADITIONAL FLOWER OF THE MONTH

September   *Morning Glory*
October   *Hop*
November   *Chrysanthemum*

FESTIVALS

Harvest Thanksgiving
Michaelmas   *29th September*
Halloween   *31st October*
Bonfire Night   *5th November*
Remembrance Day   *11th November*
Columbus Day   *October*
Thanksgiving Day   *November*

COLOUR OF THE MONTH

September   *Silver*
October   *Pale Blue*
November   *Deep Red*

September

Applecake

Ingredients

Soft Margarine	145g	(5oz)
Caster Sugar	225g	(8oz)
Fresh Egg	145g	(5oz)
Self Raising Flour	225g	(8oz)
Baking Powder	1½ Teaspoons	
Almond Essence	6 Drops	
Bramley Apples (peeled)	285g	(10oz)

○ Approximate baking time 1 hour
○ Baking temperature 170°C (325°F)
     or Gas Mark 3

Tin preparation

Well grease a 20.5cm (8") round cake tin with butter.

Method

Heat the oven to the recommended temperature.

Peel and chop the apples and place in a basin of water with a few drops of lemon juice to prevent discoloration.

Place all the ingredients, with the exception of the apple, together in a mixing bowl. Mix well with a wooden spoon.

Place some of the mixture into the well-greased tin. Strain and dry the apple and place some on to the mixture. Cover the apple with more mixture. Continue filling tin with apples and mixture until all the mixture is used. Even out the top.

Bake in the top of the oven.

After baking leave the cake in the tin for five minutes. Remove from tin on to a wire tray until cold.

Sprinkle with icing sugar.

Keep cake in a refrigerator and eat within three days of baking.

Autumn fruits

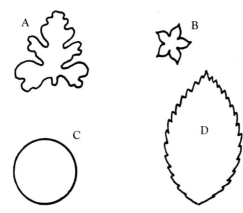

A metal or plastic cutter in each of the shapes shown is required. If a cutter is not available, the shape can be traced on to card and used as a template.

ACORN

1 Cut and bend a length of 24 gauge wire. Make a ball of flower paste. Moisten hook with egg white and insert into ball.

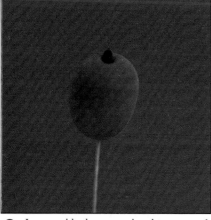

2 Insert a black stamen head into top of ball to complete the acorn nut shape.

3 Form a dome shape from flower paste. Place on a clean household sponge and hollow out centre to form an acorn cup.

4 Gently press acorn cup onto a fine cheese grater to indent the outer side of the cup.

5 Moisten the inside of the acorn cup. Insert wire stem through its centre and fix cup to the nut. Leave to dry 24 hours.

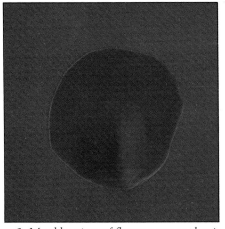

6 Mould a piece of flower paste so that it is thick at the centre and thin at the sides.

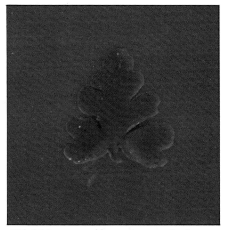

*7 Using cutter shape **A**, cut a leaf keeping the thick part at the centre of the stem.*

8 Mark the veins with the point of a cocktail stick or veiner. Cut a length of 24 gauge wire. Moisten end and insert into leaf. Leave to dry 24 hours.

9 Thinly brush leaf with edible confectioners' varnish. When dry wrap floral tape round the stem.

10 Colour acorn with edible food colour and then lightly varnish it when colour is dry.

11 Form an acorn spray from three leaves and two acorns. Bind the stems with floral tape.

BLACKBERRY BLOSSOM

12 Wind cotton around 2 fingers twelve times. Fold in two. Place 26 gauge wire on cotton and secure with floral tape. Cut ends and colour slightly.

*13 Form a cone from flower paste and flatten edge with finger and thumb. Using cutter shape **B**, cut calyx. Place on a sponge and gently curl edges.*

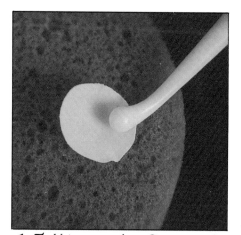

14 Moisten join in wire and insert through calyx with stamens protruding as shown. Leave to dry 24 hours.

*15 Using cutter shape **C**, cut a petal from thinly rolled flower paste. Place on clean sponge, then thin and shape edge with ball-shaped modelling tool.*

16 Moisten base of petal and fix to calyx in the position shown.

*17 Repeat step **15** four more times and fix, overlapping as shown. Leave to dry 24 hours.*

BLACKBERRY FRUIT

18 Make a ball of flower paste and insert a moistened hooked wire as in step 1.

19 Make very small beads from flower paste to form berries. Leave to dry 2 hours.

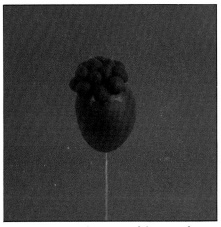

20 Moisten berries and fix into place starting at top.

21 Continue sticking on berries until the ball is completely covered. Leave to dry 24 hours. Varnish thinly and carefully.

22 Make a calyx using cutter shape B and bend the sepals backwards. Moisten and insert stem. Fix calyx to base of blackberry. Bind stem with floral tape.

23 Form a spray using leaves made in the shape of D (see page 43, steps 20-22), combined with flowers and berries.

Autumn leaves

1 *Place a sugarpaste coated cake onto two cake boards. Coat each board with royal icing. Fix ribbons as shown. Pipe bulbs around cake board base (No. 3).*

2 *Pipe a continuous rope line over each bulb (No. 1). Then overpipe the rope line (No. 1).*

3 *Pipe a decorative line on each cake board edge (No. 1).*

4 *Make (from pages 66-69) a spray of autumn fruits, flowers and leaves and fix in position on cake-top.*

5 *Outline and flood-in on waxed paper an inscription of choice. Leave to dry 24 hours. Fix to cake-top in position shown.*

6 *Pipe decorative tracery, highlighting the first and last letter of the inscription (No. 0).*

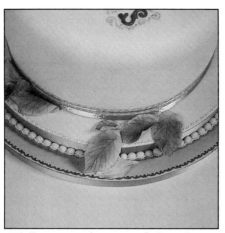

7 *Fix autumn leaves, made from flower paste, on the cake boards in the manner shown.*

8 *Pipe tracery and dots between the scattered leaves (No. 1) to complete the cake decoration.*

October

Paradise Cake

INGREDIENTS

Margarine	285g (10oz)
Caster Sugar	285g (10oz)
Fresh Egg	315g (11oz)
Plain Flour	315g (11oz)
Baking Powder	½ Teaspoon
Glacé Cherries	145g (5oz)
Angelica	60g (2oz)
Crystallised Fruits	170g (6oz)
Ground Almonds	45g (1½oz)
Almond Essence	¼ Teaspoon

○ Approximate baking time 3 hours
○ Baking temperature 150°C (300°F)
    or Gas Mark 2

TIN PREPARATION

Grease a 20.5cm (8") round tin with white fat and line it with greaseproof paper. Then grease the paper with white fat.

METHOD

Heat the oven to the recommended temperature.
Thoroughly sieve the flour and baking powder together.
Chop the cherries, angelica and fruits. Beat the margarine and sugar until light.
Beat in the egg, a little at a time.
Add the essence. Stir in the ground almonds and flour then the fruits. Mix well. Transfer to prepared tin. Bake in the centre of preheated oven.
After baking, leave the cake in the tin for thirty minutes. Then remove from tin onto a wire tray until cold.
Decorate cake with crystallised fruit and cover with a clear jelly. Use within four weeks.

Chrysanthemum

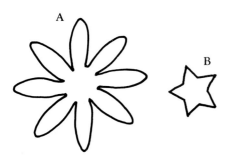

A metal or plastic cutter in each of the shapes shown is required. If a cutter is not available, the shape can be traced on to card and used as a template.

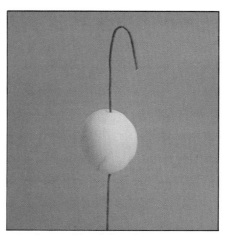

1 Cut, and bend, length of 24 gauge wire. Mould a ball from a piece of flower paste. Moisten hook with egg white and insert wire into ball.

2 Continue pushing wire through until the hook is hidden in the ball. Leave to dry 24 hours.

3 Using cutter shape A, cut a ring of petals from thinly rolled flower paste.

4 Carefully cut each petal along its centre and then separate as shown.

5 Gently roll a cocktail stick backwards and forwards over each petal to create the curled shape.

6 *Moisten the centre of the petal and insert the wire stem.*

7 *Gently fold the petals up around the ball to form flower centre.*

8 *Repeat steps 3-6 to form another petal.*

9 *Gently close petals up quite tightly around the flower.*

10 *Repeat steps 3-6. When folding the petals around the flower space loosely as shown.*

11 *Repeat steps 3-6. When folding the petal, leave more open than in step 10.*

12 Repeat steps *3-6* to complete the flower, leaving the bottom petal very loosely folded.

13 Side view of the completed flower showing the angles of the rows of petals.

14 With cutter shape **B** cut 2 calyx from thinly rolled flower paste.

15 Moisten centre of one calyx, overlay the other and fix as shown.

16 Moisten wire and insert through centre of calyx and fix into place. Leave to dry 24 hours.

17 Tint centre petals with confectioners' dusting powder. The outer petals should be slightly lighter in shade, deepening at the edges.

Cynthia

TEMPLATE

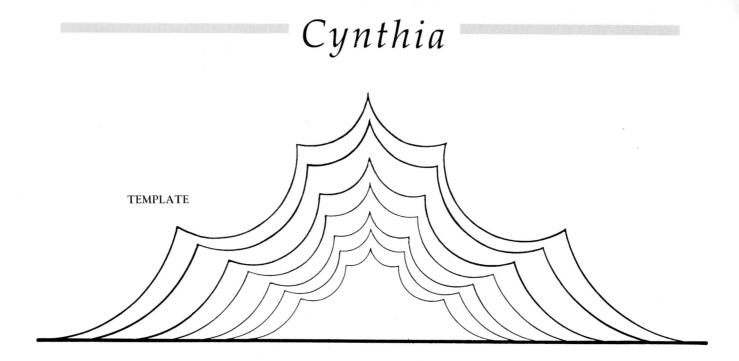

1 *Make required number of sprays of chrysanthemum flowers (see p.74-75), fill-in flowers and ribbon loops.*

2 *Pipe royal icing shells around the base of a sugarpaste coated cake and board (No. 3).*

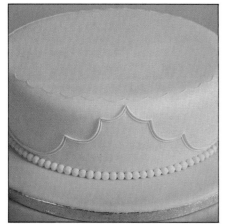

3 *Pipe the curved lines shown on cake-top (No. 1). Divide the cake into four and, using the appropriate size template as a guide, pipe the lines shown (Nos 2 and 1).*

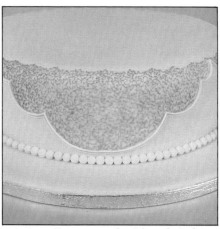

4 *Pipe filigree in each of the cake-side designs as shown (No. 0).*

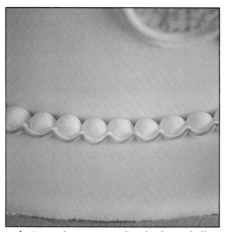

5 Pipe a line over each cake-base shell (No. 2) and then overpipe the No. 2 line (No. 1).

6 Make and fix decorative sugar doves to each cake-top quarter. Fix chrysanthemum sprays to cake-top centre and to cake-side (see main picture below).

Halloween

1 Coat a cake with sugarpaste and position on board as shown. Then coat the board.

2 Cut pieces from thinly rolled sugarpaste to form the Moon's face. Pipe shells around the cake-base (No. 1).

3 Pipe a spider on waxed paper and leave to dry 4 hours. (3 required).

4 Mould two pumpkins from sugarpaste. Decorate with cut pecans to form the stems and sugarpaste eyes and mouth.

5 Cut two ghost shapes from thinly rolled sugarpaste as shown. Frill the bottom edge by rolling a cocktail stick backwards and forwards.

6 Fix ghosts and pumpkins in position on cake-top.

7 *Pipe Halloween inscription, as shown, on cake-top and side (No. 2).*

8 *Pipe spiders' webs on side of cake (No. 0). Fix spiders on the cake board as shown in the picture below. Decorate cake board edge with ribbon.*

Dundee Cake

INGREDIENTS

Butter	225g	(8oz)
Soft Brown Sugar	225g	(8oz)
Fresh Egg	225g	(8oz)
Fresh Milk	1½ Teaspoons	
Self Raising Flour	285g	(10oz)
Mixed Spice	Pinch	
Salt	Pinch	
Currants	225g	(8oz)
Sultanas	225g	(8oz)
Chopped Peel	85g	(3oz)
Glacé Cherries	60g	(2oz)

Blanched, Split Almonds for decoration.

○ Approximate baking time 2½ hours
○ Baking temperature 180°C (350°F)
　　　　or Gas Mark 4

TIN PREPARATION

Grease a 20.5cm (8″) round tin with white fat and line it with greaseproof paper. Then grease the paper with white fat.

METHOD

Heat the oven to the recommended temperature.
Sieve together the flour, spice and salt.
Beat the butter and sugar until light and fluffy.
Beat in the eggs a little at a time with a tablespoon of the sieved flour.
Beat in the milk and a little flour.
Stir in the fruit and the rest of the flour.
Put the mixture into the prepared tin and arrange the almonds on top.
Bake at 180°C (350F°) or Gas Mark 4, for 1 hour, then cover with paper and bake at 150°C (310°F) or Gas Mark 2, for a further 1½ hours.
After baking leave the cake in the tin for thirty minutes. Then remove cake from tin and place on to a wire rack until cold. Wrap in waxed paper and allow to mature for three days.

Lily

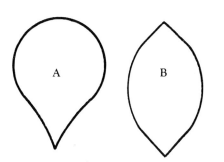

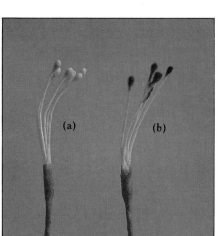

A metal or plastic cutter in each of the shapes shown is required. If a cutter is not available, the shape can be traced on to card and used as a template.

1 (**a**) *Fold 3 stamens in half and place at the end of a length of 24 gauge wire. Tape joint. (**b**) Colour stamen tips with confectioners' dusting powder.*

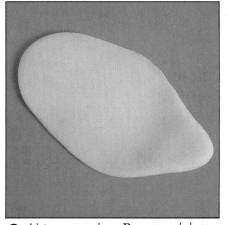

*2 Using cutter shape **B**, cut petal shape from thinly rolled flower paste. (Make base of the petal slightly thicker).*

3 Cut a length of 24 gauge wire. Moisten end of wire with egg white and insert into base of petal.

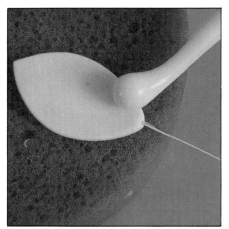

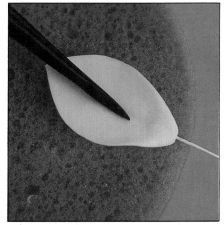

4 Place petal on a clean household sponge and thin the edge, using a ball shaped modelling tool.

5 Using the end of a cocktail stick, score along the petal's centre in a straight line.

6 Place petal on a curved surface and leave to dry 24 hours. Repeat steps *2-6* to make two further petals. Leave to dry for 24 hours.

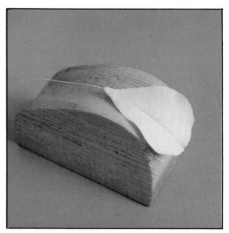

7 Using cutter shape **A**, repeat steps *2-6* to make and shape three petals. Leave to dry for 24 hours.

8 With a clean, fine and soft artists' brush, colour **B** shape petals with confectioners' dusting powder, as shown.

9 Delicately colour lines on one of the **B** petals as shown.

10 Brush lines on remaining two **B** petals, as shown, using edible food colouring.

11 Lightly colour the three **A** shaped petals, as shown, using edible food colouring.

12 Tape a petal from step **10** to the stem so that the stamens protrude outwards.

13 Tape the second petal from step **10**, overlapping slightly as shown, to the stem.

14 Tape the petal from step **9** below stamens as shown.

15 Tape one petal from step **11** behind the top petals.

16 Tape remaining two petals from step **11**, behind the other petals, as shown.

17 Flowers can be coloured in a variety of ways to match any colour scheme.

1 Make and fix lily flowers (see pages 81-83) to the edge of a heart-shaped coated cake. Decorate with strings of pearls.

2 Using a crimped round cutter, cut flower shapes from thinly rolled sugarpaste. Shape as shown. Dust with confectioners' dusting powder.

3 Fix sugarpaste flowers around the remaining cake-top edge in graduated colours.

4 Pipe a pearl in the centre of each flower (No. 2).

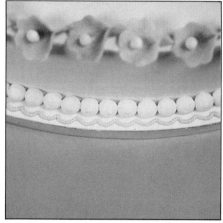

5 Pipe bulbs around the cake-base (No. 3).

6 Pipe a rope line on the cake board next to the bulbs (No. 2).

7 Pipe inscription of choice on the cake-top (No. 1).

8 Pipe delicate tracery around the inscription (No. 0) and decorate with sugar doves.

Guy Fawkes

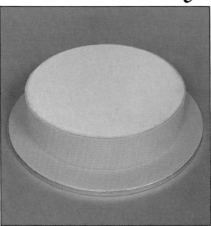

1 Coat a round cake and board with royal icing in two colours as shown.

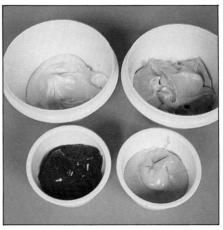

2 Colour sufficient royal icing to cover the cake-top in four separate bowls.

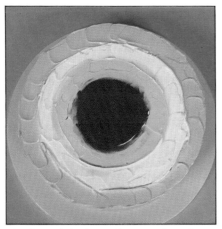

3 Spread the four colours on the cake-top as quickly as possible.

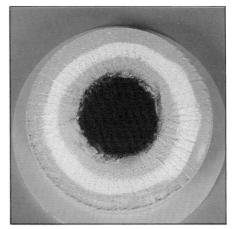

4 Immediately stipple the cake-top with a fine sponge so that the colours merge together as shown.

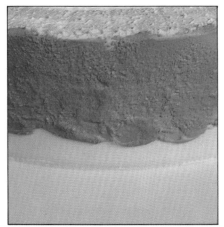

5 Spread, and stipple, blue-coloured royal icing around the top of the cake-side to represent the sky.

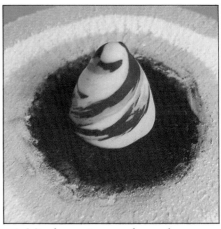

6 Mix three separate colours of sugarpaste and mould to shape shown.

7 Place chocolate fingers and flakes around the outside of the sugarpaste to form the bonfire.

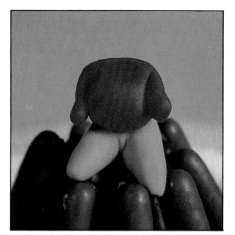

8 Make a sugarpaste body and trousers and fix to the top of the fire.

9 Make and fix head and hat. Push a chocolate finger into the centre of the bonfire for support. Decorate as shown (No. 1).

10 Pipe inscription of choice around the fire (No. 2) and then overpipe the inscription (No. 1).

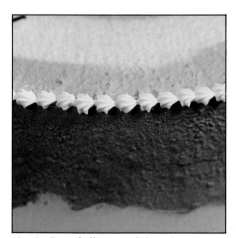

11 Pipe shells around the cake-top edge (No. 5).

12 Make, and decorate, a quantity of sugarpaste cones to represent roman candles, and a pot for 'Penny for the Guy'.

13 Fix roman candles around the cake-top.

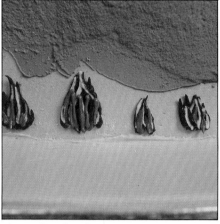

14 Pipe bonfires in several colours around the cake-base (No. 1).

15 Pipe shells below the bonfires around the cake-base (No. 2).

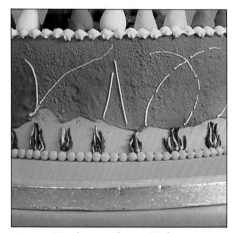

16 Pipe lines and tracery above bonfires to represent shooting fireworks (No. 1).

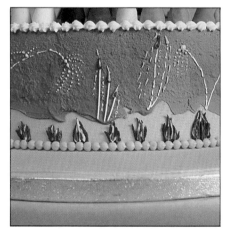

17 Pipe dots and dotted lines to illustrate fireworks bursting in the night sky (No. 1).

18 Pipe a variety of fireworks around the cake board (No. 1).

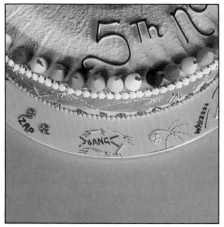

19 Pipe firework-noise words between the fireworks on the cake board and decorate with appropriate lines (No. 1).

20 Fix the 'Penny for the Guy' pot and bundles of chopped chocolate finger and flake to the cake-top. Fix colourful ribbons around the cake board edge.

Winter

*T*HE *dark days of winter lend themselves to trying out new cake recipes for tea by a warm fire, and the festivals of winter offer the cake decorator the opportunity and the challenge to create exciting new shapes and designs, or to recreate traditional favourites.*

The exotic flowers of winter are the orchids, lilies and the flame-like Poinsetta, with its brilliant splash of colour at Christmas, around which Mary designed a special cake. She also brings the past up to date with her appealing Victorian children motif, and decorates an unusually shaped Christmas cake in a traditional manner.

The romantic cake decorator is presented with the ideal opportunity for sentimental 'hearts and flowers' designs on Valentine's Day — a day which indicates that new life is stirring again and that winter will soon give way to Spring as the cycle of the seasons moves on once again.

TRADITIONAL FLOWER OF THE MONTH

December   *Holly*
January   *Snowdrop*
February   *Primrose*

FESTIVALS

Christmas Eve   *24th December*
Christmas Day   *25th December*
Boxing Day   *26th December*
New Year's Eve   *31st December*
Wassail Eve   *5th January*
Epiphany   *6th January*
Burns Night   *25th January*
Carnation Day   *29th January*
Candlemass   *1st February*
Valentine's Day   *14th February*

COLOUR OF THE MONTH

December   *Purple*
January   *Dark Green*
February   *Electric Blue*

December

Rich Fruit Cake

Ingredients

Butter	170g	(6oz)
Soft Brown Sugar	85g	(3oz)
Caster Sugar	85g	(3oz)
Ground Almonds	85g	(3oz)
Fresh Egg	225g	(8oz)
Plain Flour	225g	(8oz)
Baking Powder	½ Teaspoon	
Salt	Pinch	
Mixed Spice	½ Teaspoon	
Nutmeg	½ Teaspoon	
Glacé Cherries (chopped)	60g	(2oz)
Currants	85g	(3oz)
Sultanas	170g	(6oz)
Raisins	170g	(6oz)
Mixed Peel	85g	(3oz)
Brandy	30g	(1oz)

○ Approximate baking time 3 hours
○ Baking temperature 150°C (300°F)
  or Gas Mark 2

Tin preparation

Grease a 20.5cm (8″) round tin with white fat, and line it with greaseproof paper. Then grease the paper with white fat.

Method

Heat the oven to the recommended temperature.
Sieve together the flour, baking powder, spices and salt.
Beat the butter and sugar until light and fluffy.
Beat in the eggs a little at a time with a tablespoon of the sieved flour. Stir in the Ground Almonds.
Fold the remaining flour into the batter and then the fruit and brandy.
Spread the mixture into the prepared tin.
Bake in the centre of the oven. (Cover with greaseproof paper if the top becomes too brown).
After baking leave the cake in the tin for thirty minutes. Then remove cake from tin and place on to a wire rack until cold. Wrap in waxed paper and allow to mature for three days.

Father Christmas

1 Mould a sugarpaste ball and a tall cone. Cut a sugarpaste star. Moisten with egg white, and fasten together. Pipe eyes, nose, mouth and hat bobble (No. 1). 6 heads required.

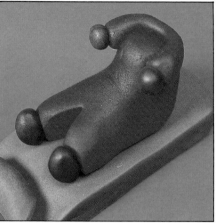

2 Mould a flat slab of sugarpaste to form a sleigh with a curled end. Mould a sugarpaste body, with a 'sausage' for arms, and balls for feet and hands. Moisten and fix into place.

3 Make a head with hat as in step *1*, moisten and fix to body. Pipe face, beard, coat, trouser trimmings, buttons and hat trimmings (No. 1).

4 Using holly shaped crimpers, carefully press into sugarpaste coated board around outer edge. Pipe shells around cake-base (No. 5).

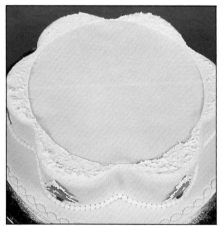

5 Cut six Christmas trees and stems. Moisten and fix. Pipe snow on trees. Cover cake-centre with paper template. Apply royal icing and stipple with a fine sponge.

6 Place Santa in the cake-centre. Stipple snow around sleigh. Decorate with sugar bells and parcels.

7 Pipe 'Christmas' alongside the snow on alternate petals (No. 1).

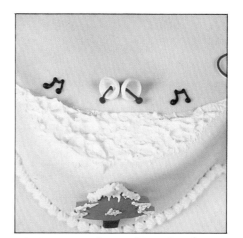

8 Pipe musical notes (No. 1) and decorate with sugar bells on alternate petals. Fix heads around cake-base and ribbons to cake board edge.

Mistletoe

TEMPLATE

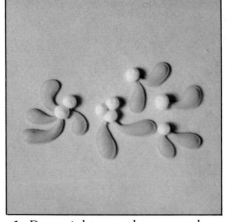

1 Draw mistletoe template onto card. Place waxed paper over template, outline and fill-in leaves using royal icing without glycerine (No. 0). Pipe berries (No. 1).

2 Trace boy and girl template onto card. Place waxed paper over template. Using a piping bag without a tube, fill-in faces and socks.

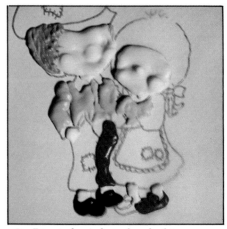

3 Pipe-in boy's hair, hand, shirt (excluding the collar) trouser leg and shoes. Then fill-in the girl's bodice and shoe as shown.

4 *Pipe-in girl's hair and second shoe, and the boy's trouser leg and shirt cuff.*

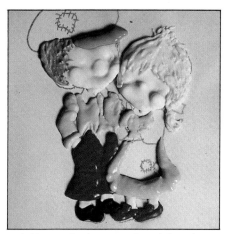

5 *Pipe-in boy's cap peak and then the girl's dress.*

6 *Pipe-in boy's braces and then the girl's apron.*

7 *Pipe-in boy's tie, shirt collar and top of hat, and then the girl's arms and hands.*

8 *Pipe-in girl's flower, hair ribbon and collar. Decorate apron with piped dots. Leave to dry 24 hours.*

9 *With edible food colouring paint face features, stripes on boy's tie, collar, cuffs and patch on boy's trousers. Pipe buttons on boy's shoes and braces.*

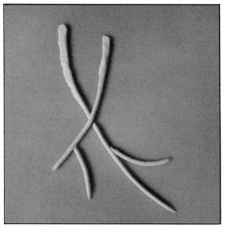

10 Pipe a scalloped line around a heart-shaped cake and board edge, using royal icing without glycerine (No. 2). Flood-in with softened royal icing. Leave to dry 24 hours.

11 Pipe mistletoe branches with a piping bag without a tube, using royal icing.

12 Carefully remove mistletoe from waxed paper and fix to branches. Remove boy and girl and fix on cake-top. Pipe snow below boy and girl.

13 Pipe inscription of choice (No. 2). Then overpipe inscription (No. 1).

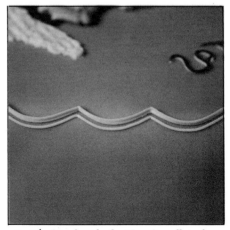

14 Pipe plain shells around cake-base (No. 3). Pipe a scalloped line around the cake-top edge (No. 2).

15 Pipe beside the No. 2 scalloped line (No. 1). Then overpipe the No. 2 scalloped line (No. 1).

16 Pipe criss-cross lines on cake-top to form snow flakes (No. 1).

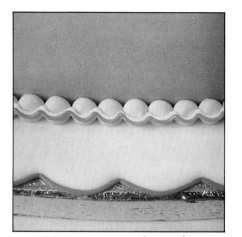

17 Pipe a continuous line on the cake-base shells (No. 2). Then overpipe the No. 2 line against the first line (No. 1).

Poinsettia

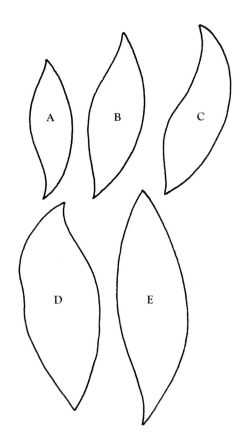

NUMBER OF LEAVES REQUIRED:

Shape A   ×4 RED
Shape B   ×2 RED
Shape C   ×2 RED
Shape D   ×3 RED
Shape E   ×3 RED
Shape E   ×3 GREEN

A metal or plastic cutter in each of the shapes shown
is required. If a cutter is not available, the shape can
be traced on to card and used as a template.

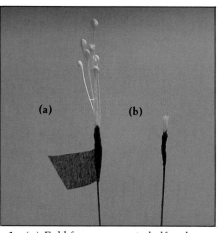

1 (a) *Fold four stamens in half and
twist 24 gauge wire around the centre.
Tape join as shown.* (b) *Cut stamen heads
off approximately 5mm (¼″) above the
tape.*

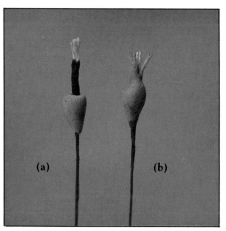

2 (a) *Mould a cone from flower paste.
Moisten tape with egg white and insert
wire into cone.* (b) *Mould cone as shown.
Leave to dry 24 hours.*

3 *Repeat steps 1-3 to form six more
flower heads. Pipe two royal icing dots
on each flower head (No. 1). Leave to dry
1 hour. Bind stems together with floral
tape.*

4 *Cut out a leaf from thinly rolled
flower paste. Place leaf on a
household sponge and mark the veins with
light pressure from a cocktail stick.*

5 Cut a length of 26 gauge wire and lay on leaf. Pinch moistened leaf base on to wire. Leave to dry 24 hours. Repeat steps *5-7* for the required number of leaf shapes.

6 Brush leaves and flower heads with confectioners' dusting powder. Tape **A** leaves to the flower stem. Then tape **B** leaves, followed by **C** leaves.

7 Continue taping red **D** leaves to the stem. Then add red **E** leaves and finally the green **E** leaves to complete the flower.

8 Cover cake with sugarpaste and carefully crimp the edge on the cake board.

9 Fix the spray in a suitable position. Pipe 'Christmas', or inscription of choice, with royal icing (No. 2).

10 Carefully overpipe the inscription (No. 1) in a strong, dark colour.

11 *Pipe beside inscription as shown (No. 0). Decorate with piped holly leaves and berries (No. 0).*

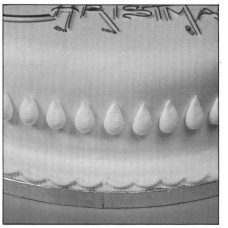

12 *Pipe large, plain elongated shells evenly spaced around the middle of the cake-side (No. 3).*

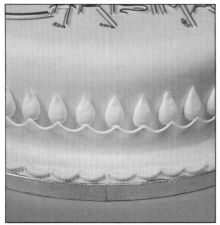

13 *Pipe a line at the base of each shell to join shells with loops (No. 2).*

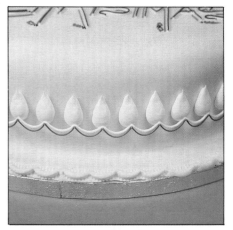

14 *Pipe a second line below the first line to form another row of loops (No. 1). (Attach at top of each loop).*

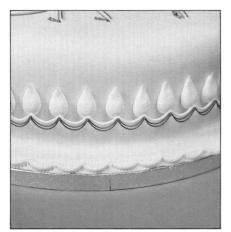

15 *Pipe a third row of loops below the second line (No. 1). (Attach at top of each loop).*

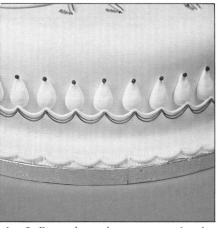

16 *Pipe a dot at the top centre of each cake-side shell (No. 1).*

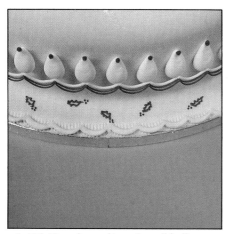

17 *Pipe the outline of small holly leaves and then dots for berries around the cake board (No. 0).*

18 *Make and fix a sugarpaste log to the cake-top. Decorate with piped snow and robins. Fix ribbon around the cake board edge to complete the cake.*

Greetings

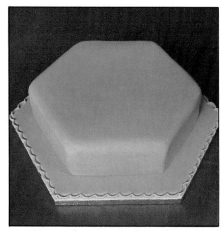

1 Cover a hexagonal cake and board in sugarpaste. Crimp the sugarpaste around the cake board edge.

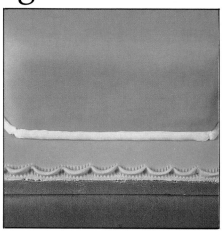

2 Pipe a line round cake-base with royal icing (No. 44).

3 Pipe an 'S' scroll from one corner to centre of one side of cake-top edge (No. 44).

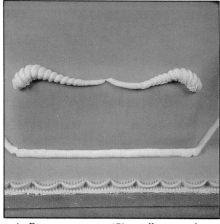

4 Pipe an opposite 'S' scroll to match (No. 44).

5 Pipe a 'C' scroll from left to centre (No. 44).

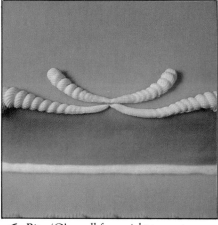

6 Pipe 'C' scroll from right to centre (No. 44).

7 Pipe right and left 'S' scrolls at cake-base (No. 44). Repeat steps *3-7* on each side.

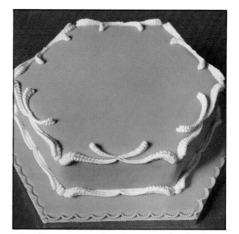

8 Overpipe each cake-top and cake-base scroll (No. 3).

9 Overpipe each cake-top and cake-base scroll (No. 2).

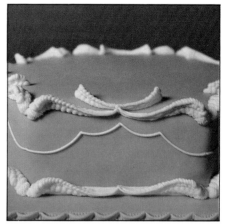

10 Pipe a curved line around the cake-side as shown (No. 2).

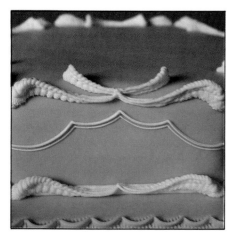

11 Pipe a line beneath the line, and then against the No. 2 line (No. 1).

12 Pipe inscription of choice on the cake-top centre (No. 2).

13 Overpipe the inscription with a contrasting colour (No. 1).

14 Pipe tracery as shown (No. 1), keeping the tube on the cake-top surface.

15 Pipe further tracery and dots around the inscription (No. 1).

16 Overpipe each cake-top and cake-base scroll (No. 1).

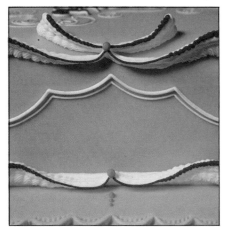

17 Pipe a dot at each scroll centre point and then graduated dots at the centre of all cake board sides (No. 1).

18 Make and fix a spray of bells, leaves and ribbon loops to the cake-top.

19 Fix a bell to the centre of each cake-top side.

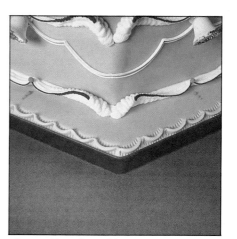

20 Fix velvet ribbon around edge of cake board to complete the decoration.

January

Ginger Cake

INGREDIENTS

Plain Flour	285g (10oz)
Baking Powder	7g (¼oz)
Ginger	7g (¼oz)
Caster Sugar	60g (2oz)
Butter	115g (4oz)
Fresh Egg	170g (6oz)
Milk	85g (3oz)
Syrup	340g (12oz)
Stem ginger (chopped)	115g (4oz)

○ Approximate baking time 1 hour
○ Baking temperature 180°C (350°)
     or Gas Mark 4

TIN PREPARATION

Grease a 20.5cm (8″) round tin with white fat, and line it with greaseproof paper. Then grease the paper with white fat.

METHOD

Heat the oven to the recommended temperature.

Sieve together the flour, baking powder and ginger. Stir in the sugar.

Rub in the butter until the mixture resembles fine breadcrumbs. Mix together the syrup, eggs and milk and add to the other ingredients.

Mix until smooth and clear. Fold in the stem ginger.

Put mixture into the prepared tin. Bake in the centre of the oven.

After baking, leave the cake in the tin for thirty minutes. Then remove from tin onto a wire tray until cold.

Decorate with stem ginger and a cherry to form flower. Use within three days of making.

Nella

NELLA'S TEMPLATE

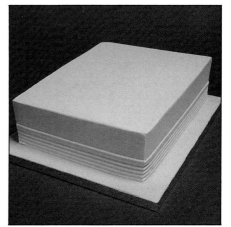

1 Coat an oblong cake in almond paste and royal icing. On the last coating of the sides, use a scraper to create the effect shown. Then coat the board.

2 Trace Nella's template on to card. Cover template with waxed paper. Pipe-in the parts shown with royal icing.

3 Continue to carefully pipe-in the further parts as shown.

4 Complete piping-in remaining parts as shown. Leave to dry 24 hours. Brush-in eyes and the markings shown with edible food colouring.

5 Roll brightly coloured sugarpaste into balloons for cake-edge.

6 Pipe barrel scrolls around the cake-base (No. 43).

7 Carefully remove elephant from waxed paper and fix in place. Form three balloons from sugarpaste. Fix into place and pipe 'strings' to elephant's hands (No. 1).

8 Pipe inscription of choice on the cake-top (No. 1).

9 Fix sugarpaste balloons around cake-edge as shown.

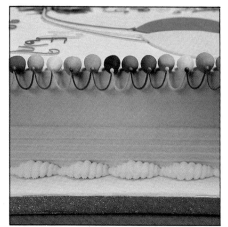

10 Pipe a different coloured loop to link each balloon. Then pipe a dot at each loop join (No. 1).

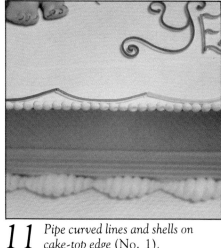

11 Pipe curved lines and shells on cake-top edge (No. 1).

12 Pipe curved lines and shells around cake board edge (No. 1).

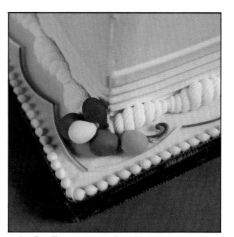

13 Decorate each cake-base corner with sugarpaste balloons and piped dots and strings (No. 1).

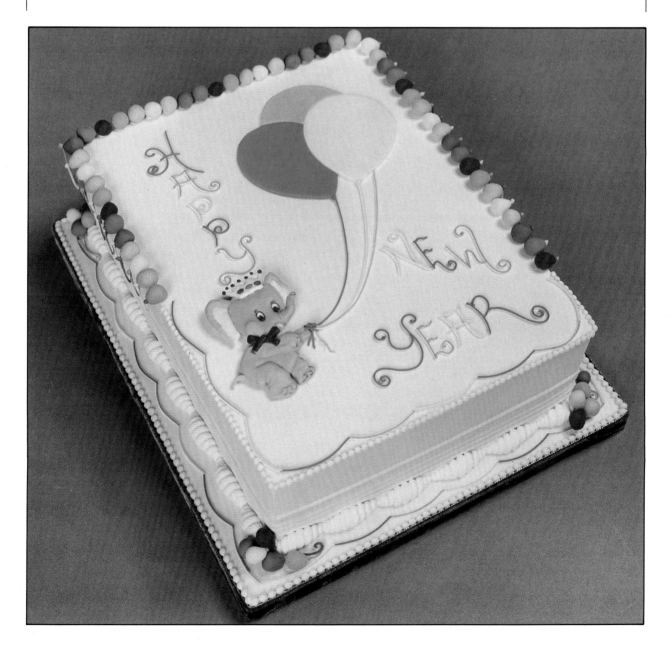

Jeremy

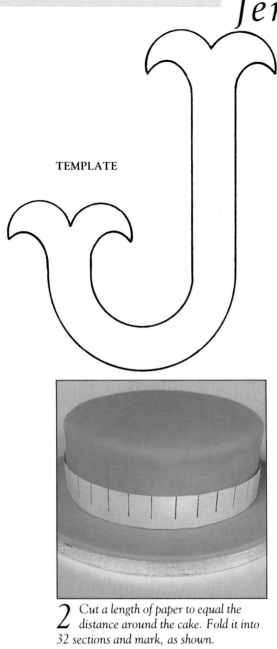

TEMPLATE

1 Cover a round cake and board with sugarpaste.

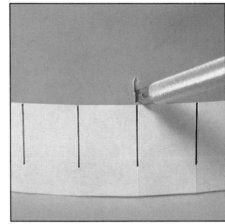

2 Cut a length of paper to equal the distance around the cake. Fold it into 32 sections and mark, as shown.

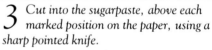

3 Cut into the sugarpaste, above each marked position on the paper, using a sharp pointed knife.

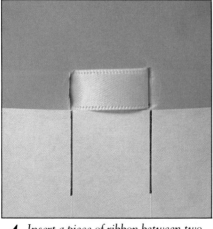

4 Insert a piece of ribbon between two cuts, as shown, to form a loop.

5 Continue to insert ribbon pieces until each section is completed.

6 *Trace and cut out a template in the initial required. Place it on the cake-top and pipe a line, with royal icing, around it (No. 2).*

7 *Carefully remove the template. Decorate with piped filigree, dots and petals (No. 0).*

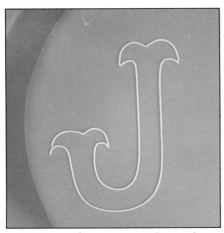

8 *Complete piping name of choice (No. 1), then decorate as shown (No. 0).*

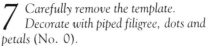

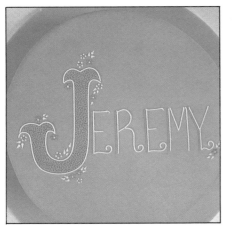

9 *Pipe scrolls along part of the cake-top edge, as shown (No. 42).*

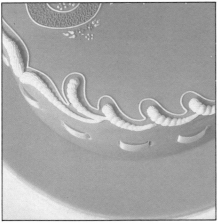

10 *Pipe a line beside each cake-top scroll (No. 2).*

11 *Pipe curved lines around remaining cake-top edge to form the scallop shown (No. 2).*

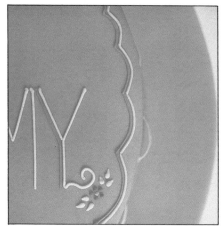

12 Pipe a line beside No. 2 scalloped line (No. 1).

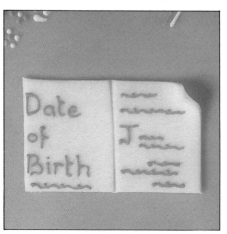

13 Make, decorate and fix a sugarpaste birth announcement as shown.

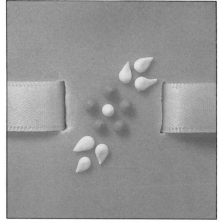

14 Pipe dots and petals between each piece of ribbon on cake-side (No. 2).

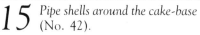

15 Pipe shells around the cake-base (No. 42).

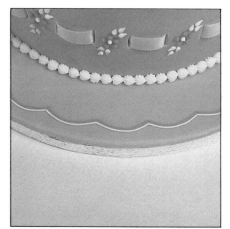

16 Pipe a curved line around the cake board edge (No. 2). Then pipe a line beside the No. 2 line (No. 1).

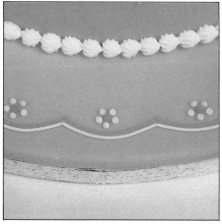
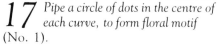

17 Pipe a circle of dots in the centre of each curve, to form floral motif (No. 1).

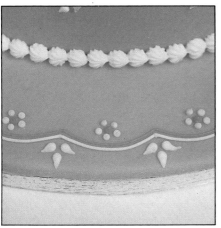

18 Pipe petal shapes at each curved line join (No. 1).

19 Fix baby to cake-top and decorate around it with tracery and dots (No. 1).

February

Chocolate Sponge Cake

INGREDIENTS

Butter	225g	(8oz)
Caster Sugar	225g	(8oz)
Fresh Egg (separated)	285g	(10oz)
Plain Flour (sieved)	170g	(6oz)
Cocoa Powder (sieved)	60g	(2oz)
Baking Powder (sieved)	1 Teaspoon	

○ Approximate baking time 14 minutes

○ Baking temperature 200°C (400°F)
or Gas Mark 6

TIN PREPARATION

Grease two 20.5cm (8″) round sponge tins with white fat and then sprinkle sufficient flour into the tin to cover the inside. Gently shake the tin to ensure the fat is covered with flour, then tap out any excess.

METHOD

Heat the oven to the recommended temperature.

Beat the butter and sugar until light and fluffy. Add the egg yolks a little at a time and beat well.

Lightly fold into the batter the sieved flour, cocoa powder and baking powder. Whisk the egg whites and fold into the batter.

Divide the mixture evenly between the two tins and bake in the middle of the preheated oven.

After baking, leave the cake in the tins for five minutes. Then remove and place on a wire tray until cold.

Wrap cake in waxed paper and store in deep-freeze for up to six months. Use within three days of baking or after defrosting.

The cake can be sandwiched together with buttercream and the top dusted with icing sugar and cocoa powder.

Chris

TEMPLATE

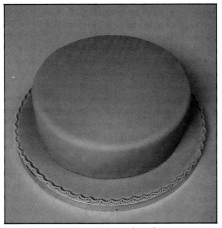

1 Cover cake and board with sugarpaste and then immediately crimp the paste, along the cake board edge.

2 Using template as guide, pipe a decorative 'C', or initial of choice, on waxed paper with royal icing (No. 1). Leave to dry 24 hours.

3 Using template as guide pipe the fan shape shown on waxed paper (No. 1). 24 are required. Leave to dry 24 hours.

4 Pipe plain shells around cake-base (No. 2).

5 Divide cake-top edge into 12 sections. Fix a piped fan at each mark. Ensure fans do not protrude further than the cake board.

6 *Fix remaining 12 fans around the cake board edge, positioning them between each upper fan.*

7 *Fix the 'C' to cake-top and pipe remaining letters of name in the style shown (No. 1).*

8 *Pipe a series of straight lines as shown (No. 1).*

9 *Carefully pipe the further lines shown (No. 1).*

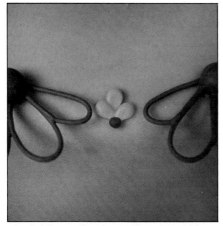

10 *Pipe a floral motif between each cake top fan (No. 1).*

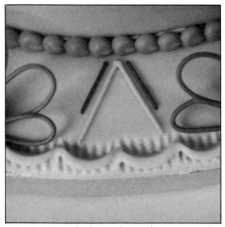

11 *Pipe the lines shown between each fan, around the cake board edge (No. 1).*

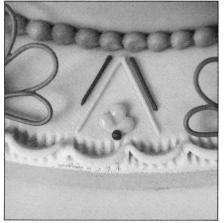

12 Pipe a floral motif inside each cake board pattern (No. 1).

13 Fix decorations of choice to cake-top.

Valentine

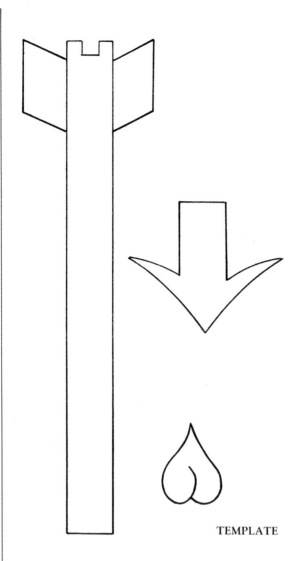

TEMPLATE

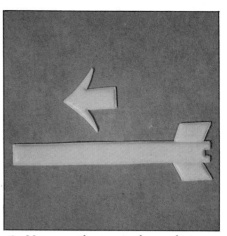

1 Using templates as guides, outline on waxed paper the arrow shaft and head (No. 2) using royal icing without glycerine. Then flood-in. Leave to dry 24 hours.

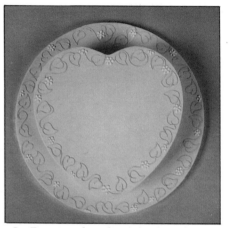

2 Decorate the cake-top and board with heart shaped design as shown, using the heart template as a guide (No. 1).

3 Pipe shells around the cake-top edge and base (No. 42).

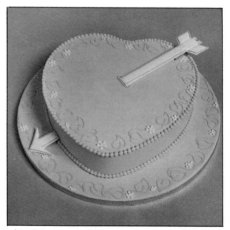

4 Fix arrow shaft to cake-top and head to cake-base at a downward sloping angle.

5 Pipe inscription of choice on cake-top and then decorate inscription with piped tracery (No. 1).

6 Fix ribbon bow held by sugar doves to cake-top and pipe-in kisses (No. 1).

Index/Glossary